Contents

The Aitareya Upanishad does not elaborate on Vamadeva's life after this realisation, but the importance of his story lies in the profound wisdom he attained. This knowledge freed him from the

PREFACE

The Upanishads have captivated spiritual seekers for millennia, offering profound insights into the nature of existence, consciousness, and the ultimate reality. their timeless wisdom transcends religious boundaries, presenting truths that resonate universally with anyone yearning to understand life's deeper mysteries. despite their significance, the teachings of the Upanishads often feel distant and abstract to modern readers. written in ancient, dense Sanskrit verses, these texts can be difficult to interpret without guidance.

This book is born out of the desire to bring the Upanishads closer to today's audience, to make their profound teachings more approachable, relatable, and, most importantly, liveable. While the teachings in the Upanishads are universal, they often express truths that may seem elusive or overly philosophical when encountered for the first time. Through carefully chosen stories that illustrate these teachings, I hope to unravel the depth of these ancient texts and present them in a way that speaks to both the intellect and the heart.

The stories woven into the fabric of this book are not merely for entertainment. They serve as tools for deeper understanding, mirrors reflecting the truths contained in the Upanishadic teachings. Whether it's a young boy learning the nature of death from the god Yama, or a sage meditating on the sound of Om these stories bring the eternal wisdom of the Upanishads into a space where modern readers can grasp their meaning and relevance.

Each chapter of this book pairs a core teaching from the Upanishads with a corresponding story that not only explains the teaching but also shows how it plays out in the lives of those who seek to know the eternal truths. The aim is to offer a bridge between the metaphysical and the practical, showing how the lofty ideas of the Upanishads can be applied to our everyday existence.

This book is not just for scholars or theologians to analyse—it is for anyone who is on a journey of self-discovery, who seeks answers to life's biggest questions: Who am I? What is my purpose? How do I find peace in an ever-changing world?

The Upanishads provide answers, not in the form of rigid dogma, but in a way that allows for personal reflection and spiritual growth. The teachings are as relevant today as they were thousands of years ago, offering guidance on how to transcend the illusions of the material world, understand the true nature of the self, and realise the ultimate reality—Brahman.

As you turn the pages of this book, I invite you to explore these teachings not only with your mind but with your heart. Reflect on the stories, meditate on the ideas, and allow the wisdom of the Upanishads to unfold within you. This book is not the end of the journey, but the beginning of your own exploration into the infinite truth that lies at the heart of all existence.

May the wisdom of the Upanishads guide you on your path, and may the stories within inspire you to live with greater awareness, compassion, and understanding.

In gratitude and reverence,

Rohit Tikoo

OVERVIEW OF THE UPANISHADS

The Upanishads stand as the cornerstone of Hindu philosophy, providing a deep well of metaphysical insights and spiritual guidance. These ancient texts, considered the final segment of the Vedas, are also referred to as Vedanta—literally meaning "the culmination of the Vedas." Unlike the earlier portions of the Vedas, which primarily focus on rituals and sacrificial rites, the Upanishads mark a philosophical shift towards inward exploration, meditation, and the quest for self-realisation. Their wisdom invites us to move beyond mere external practices and direct our attention toward the internal journey of understanding the self and the universe.

Composed between 800 and 500 BCE, the Upanishads emphasise understanding the core principles of existence—Brahman (the ultimate reality), Atman (the self), and the purpose of human life. Where the earlier Vedic texts celebrated the worship of deities through rituals, the Upanishads usher in a more contemplative approach, challenging us to seek the unity between the individual soul and the universal consciousness. This shift represents not just a change in philosophy but a transformative journey towards higher awareness and enlightenment.

The key concepts of the Upanishads can be understood through the following core ideas:

- Brahman: The infinite, formless essence that is the source of all existence. Everything emerges from Brahman, and in time, everything returns to it. Brahman is beyond time, space, and all physical limitations, making it both immanent and transcendent.
- Atman: The innermost self or soul of every individual, identical to Brahman. This realisation—that the true self is not the body, mind, or ego but the divine Atman— is at the heart of Upanishadic teaching.
- Moksha: The ultimate liberation from the endless cycle of birth, death, and rebirth (samsara). Attaining Moksha means recognizing the self's true nature and becoming one with Brahman.
- Karma: The law of cause and effect that governs existence. Every action we take leaves a trace, which shapes our future experiences. Understanding this law helps

one live a life aligned with spiritual principles.

- Maya: The illusion or veil that clouds our perception of reality. Maya makes us believe that the material world is all there is, leading us to identify with our physical forms and egos. Transcending Maya is essential for realising the unity of Atman and Brahman.

The teachings of the Upanishads are presented in various forms—dialogues between sages and disciples, allegorical stories, and direct philosophical discourses. This variety offers readers and seekers multiple entry points to engage with their profound wisdom. The stories are often simple yet carry deeply layered meanings that challenge the seeker to go beyond surface understanding and reflect on life's deeper truths.

The relevance of the Upanishads is timeless, and their influence extends far beyond the borders of India. Their ideas have shaped not only the Vedantic tradition but have also resonated with scholars, mystics, and philosophers worldwide. At their core, the Upanishads pose questions that continue to resonate today: Who am I? What is the purpose of life? What is the nature of reality?

For spiritual seekers, students, parents, children, and philosophers, the Upanishads offer a guiding light on the path to wisdom, encouraging us to transcend the mundane and connect with the infinite.

THE HARD PROBLEM OF CONSCIOUSNESS

Consciousness, that mysterious thread weaving through our every experience, has intrigued humanity for millennia. It is a puzzle that evens the sharpest minds of modern science struggle to unravel. In today's world, we often speak of the "hard problem of consciousness," a phrase coined by philosopher David Chalmers to describe the difficulty of explaining how subjective experience arises from the physical brain. How does matter produce mind? How does the arrangement of neurons and chemical processes give rise to our inner world of thoughts, feelings, and sensations?

Surprisingly, the ancient Upanishads—texts written thousands of years ago—already engaged deeply with the essence of consciousness, addressing questions that remain relevant today. For the sages of the Upanishads, consciousness was not a mere byproduct of physical processes but the very foundation of reality itself. To them, the inner self (Atman) was identical to the ultimate reality (Brahman). And it is through this lens that they approached what we today might call the "hard problem" of consciousness.

What is Consciousness?

The Upanishads assert that consciousness is not just a part of the universe but its very essence. In the Mandukya Upanishad, for instance, we find a profound exploration of the states of consciousness: waking, dreaming, deep sleep, and the state of pure awareness, called Turiya. According to the sages, these states are not distinct entities, but varying manifestations of one undivided consciousness.

In modern science, we often view consciousness as something that arises from the brain, an "emergent property" of complex physical processes. But the Upanishads suggest the opposite—that consciousness is fundamental. It doesn't arise from the brain; rather, the brain operates within consciousness. This flips the modern materialistic understanding on its head.

The sages understood consciousness as Chit, the sentient principle that pervades the cosmos. According to the Brihadaranyaka Upanishad, "Consciousness is Brahman." This means consciousness is not a phenomenon limited to individual beings but is the universal ground of existence. While modern science searches for the biological roots of consciousness, the Upanishads claim that the mystery lies not in neurons or synapses, but in the very nature of being itself.

The Illusion of Separation

One of the key problems with understanding consciousness is the persistent illusion that it is tied to individual identity. We think of "my" consciousness as distinct from "yours" or from the world around us. This dualistic way of thinking—me and the world—forms the foundation of much of Western philosophy and science.

The Upanishads radically challenge this assumption. According to the sages, the idea that we are separate, isolated beings is a delusion, one that traps us in ignorance (Avidya). The Chandogya Upanishad tells us: Tat Tvam Asi—"Thou art That." This profound statement declares that the individual self (Atman) is one with the ultimate reality (Brahman). There is no fundamental separation between the observer and the observed, between the individual mind and the universe.

The sages argue that this perceived separation is the root of all suffering. The more we cling to the idea that we are distinct from the world around us, the more we experience alienation, fear, and division. True knowledge (Vidya) comes when we realize that consciousness is not bound to the self but is the unifying force behind all existence.

Consciousness Beyond the Brain

In addressing the hard problem of consciousness, modern science often attempts to reduce subjective experience to brain activity. Yet, even with the most sophisticated imaging technologies, we remain unable to explain why or how the brain produces the rich tapestry of inner experience. There is a profound gap between the objective study of brain matter and the subjective nature of consciousness.

The Upanishads, however, suggest that consciousness is not an epiphenomenon of the brain but the substratum that allows all existence to unfold. In the Kena Upan shad, the seeker asks: "By whose command does the mind think? By whose power do we see and hear?" The answer given is that it is the Atman, the indwelling self, that empowers the senses and the mind. This self is not the brain or the body, but pure awareness.

This idea resonates with many spiritual traditions, but it also echoes in the questions posed by quantum physics and cosmology. Car consciousness exist independently of matter? Is it the foundational element of reality? The

Upanishads answer with a resounding "Yes." The seers believed that consciousness precedes and underpins all physical reality.

Transcending the Hard Problem

To the modern mind, the hard problem of consciousness may seem like an unsolvable riddle. How can we bridge the gap between objective brain functions and subjective experiences like the colour red, the taste of mango, or the feeling of love? The Upanishads offer a path out of this conundrum, but it is not one that can be fully grasped by intellectual understanding alone.

The solution, according to the sages, is experiential. To know the true nature of consciousness, one must move beyond intellectual inquiry and experience the state of pure awareness directly. This is where the ancient practice of meditation comes in. By quieting the mind and withdrawing from the distractions of the outer world, we can come into contact with the Turiya state—the pure, unconditioned consciousness that lies beyond waking, dreaming, and deep sleep. The concept of Turiya is discussed in detail n later chapters of this book

When we access this state, the hard problem dissolves. Consciousness is no longer seen as something that needs to be "explained" by the brain because it is revealed as the very fabric of reality. It is not something we "have"; it is what we are. This realization is the core teaching of the Upanishads. The hard problem of consciousness, which so troubles modern philosophy and neuroscience, is transformed into a pathway to spiritual awakening.

The hard problem of consciousness may seem like an insurmountable intellectual challenge, but the Upanishads offer a radically different perspective. Rather than trying to fit consciousness into the framework of materialism, they invite us to see it as the ground of all existence. The sages understood that consciousness is not a problem to be solved but a reality to be realized.

The quest to understand consciousness, then, is not just a scientific or philosophical endeavour but a spiritual one. By turning inward, we can discover that the consciousness we experience is not a fleeting product of the brain but the eternal essence of the universe itself. In this realization lies true liberation (Moksha)—the ultimate goal of human existence.

This book connects ancient wisdom with contemporary challenges, presenting the

Upanishadic teachings as a profound and enduring response to modern philosophical questions about consciousness.

PURPOSE OF THE BOOK

The Upanishads are revered as one of the most profound spiritual texts in the world, but their intricate language, abstract concepts, and symbolic expressions often make them difficult to understand. For centuries, scholars have studied these texts deeply, but many readers struggle to access their true essence without a guide to interpret and simplify their meanings. This book seeks to close that gap by making the timeless wisdom of the Upanishads accessible to modern readers.

By blending key teachings with illustrative stories, the book breathes life into the ancient wisdom of the Upanishads, enabling readers to connect with the teachings in ways that are both engaging and meaningful. Whether you are a devoted spiritual seeker or someone with a casual curiosity about the ancient texts, this book will speak to your soul and offer insights that are easy to grasp, yet profound enough to stir deep reflection.

What Makes Stories So Effective?

Storytelling has long been a powerful tool for communicating deep truths. When it comes to spiritual teachings, stories provide relatable, easy-to-understand narratives that transcend intellectual barriers, allowing readers to emotionally engage with complex ideas. The Upanishads themselves often present their wisdom through dialogues, parables, and allegories, showing that stories are essential for transmitting philosophical ideas. In this book, we harness the same tradition of storytelling to unlock the wisdom within the Upanishads.

The stories in this book are used to:

- **Simplify Complex Concepts**: Concepts like *Brahman* (the ultimate reality), *Atman* (the self), and *Moksha* (liberation) can often feel distant or too abstract for readers. Through stories, these ideas become relatable, allowing readers to grasp them in a more concrete and understandable way.
- **Engage Emotionally**: Stories allow readers to connect with spiritual teachings on a deeper emotional level. Characters, events, and plots make the teachings more vivid and real, transforming abstract principles into lived experiences.
- **Provide Practical Guidance**: By embedding Upanishadic wisdom within real-life scenarios, the book helps readers see how these ancient teachings can be applied to

modern living. The teachings are not just theoretical—they offer valuable insights on how to lead a more aware, compassionate, and fulfilled life.

- Invite Reflection: Stories often leave room for interpretation, encouraging readers to reflect on their own lives and experiences. This open-endedness deepens personal connection with the material, making it more than just something to read—it becomes a mirror for the reader's own spiritual journey.

HOW THE BOOK IS STRUCTURED

Each chapter will introduce a significant teaching from the Upanishads, explaining its philosophical significance in a clear and approachable way. This explanation will be followed by a carefully selected story or parable that brings the teaching to life, illustrating how these profound ideas manifest in relatable situations. The stories are sourced from the Upanishads themselves, the Puranas, and other traditional commentaries, ensuring that they remain authentic while offering universal appeal.

In addition to the stories, reflective questions at the end of each chapter will guide readers to think about how the teachings apply to their own lives, encouraging deeper engagement with the material. This way, readers are not only invited to understand the Upanishads intellectually but also to experience their transformative power firsthand.

Why This Book?

The purpose of this book is not just to present the teachings of the Upanishads but to serve as a bridge between ancient wisdom and the modern world. Whether you are seeking personal growth, deeper spiritual insights, or simply a window into the mysteries of life, this book offers a clear path to navigate the profound teachings of the self and the universe.

At its core, the Upanishads are not simply texts to be read and intellectually understood. They are living wisdom, meant to be realised and experienced. This book is an invitation to begin or continue your journey toward that realisation, offering the tools and guidance needed to transform the teachings of the Upanishads into a source of personal and spiritual awakening.

INTRODUCTION TO THE 108 UPANISHADS

The Upanishads are foundational texts within Hindu philosophy, offering deep insights into metaphysics, spirituality, and the nature of the self. Regarded as the culmination of Vedic wisdom, they are often called *Vedanta*, meaning "the end of the Vedas." Over time, many

Upanishads were composed, but tradition recognizes 108 of these texts as particularly significant. These 108 Upanishads have been revered across generations for their ability to guide seekers toward self-realisation and the understanding of universal truths.

The authoritative list of these 108 Upanishads is provided in the *Muktika Upanishad*, a later Upanishadic text. Within this text, Lord Rama, a central figure in Hinduism, instructs his devotee Hanuman on the spiritual importance of the Upanishads. It is during this exchange that Lord Rama reveals the list of the 108 Upanishads, further emphasising their role in achieving *moksha*—spiritual liberation. This dialogue highlights the intimate relationship between knowledge and liberation, central themes that resonate throughout all the Upanishads.

The Sacredness of the Number 108

The number 108 holds special importance within Hindu tradition. It is viewed as a sacred number, symbolising completeness and spiritual wholeness. This idea is echoed in various spiritual practices, such as the use of 108 beads in a *mala* (prayer beads) during meditation or chanting. The number is believed to represent the entirety of creation, connecting the physical with the divine, and it often appears in contexts related to self-realisation and enlightenment.

The Variety of Upanishads

While the Upanishads like *Isha*, *Kena*, *Katha*, and *Mundaka* are more widely known and studied, the full list of 108 includes a vast array of texts, each contributing uniquely to the broader philosophical and spiritual framework of Vedanta. These texts address various dimensions of existence, from the nature of reality and the self to ethical living and the path to ultimate truth, known as *Brahman*. Each Upanishad carries its own teachings and philosophical insights, adding to the rich tapestry of Hindu thought.

Tat Tvam Asi (**तत् त्वम् असि**) - The Eternal Truth of Sanatan Dharma

Sanatan Dharma, is the eternal and universal way of life that has guided countless souls towards spiritual enlightenment for millennia. At the heart of this profound philosophy lies the concept of "Tat Tvam Asi" (**तत् त्वम् असि**) - a Sanskrit phrase that encapsulates the very essence of spiritual realisation in Hindu thought.

The Origin and Meaning of Tat Tvam Asi

Tat Tvam Asi," translating to "Thou Art That" or "You are That," is one of the Mahavakyas (great sayings) found in the **Chandogya Upanishad,** part of the Sama Veda. This profound statement is at the core of Advaita Vedanta, a school of Hindu philosophy that emphasises non-dualism.

In the context of Advait Vedanta

Tat(**तत्**) refers to Brahman, the ultimate reality, the absolute and eternal truth that is the source of all existence.

Tvam (**त्वम्**) represents the individual self, the Atman, which is the eternal essence of one's being.

Asi(**असि**) is the verb that equates the two, asserting their fundamental oneness.

, "Tat Tvam Asi" expresses the non-dual nature of reality. It teaches that the individual self (Atman) and the universal self (Brahman) are one and the same. This realisation is considered the pinnacle of spiritual wisdom in Hindu philosophy.

The great proponent of Advait Vedanta **Adi Shankaracharya,** in his commentaries on the Upanishads, elaborates on this concept, explaining that the apparent difference between the individual and the absolute is due to ignorance (Avidya) and superimposition (adhyasa). When this ignorance is removed through spiritual knowledge and practice, the true nature of the self is realised.

The Four Mahavakyas

Tat Tvam Asi" is one of the four Mahavakyas, each associated with one of the four Vedas:

- 1. Prajnanam Brahma (प्रज्ञानं ब्रह्म) - "Consciousness is Brahman" (Aitareya Upanishad, Rig Veda)
- 2. Aham Brahmasmi (अहं ब्रह्मास्मि) - "I am Brahman" (Brihadaranyaka Upanishad, Yajur Veda)
- 3. Tat Tvam Asi (तत् त्वम् असि) - "Thou art That" (Chandogya Upanishad, Sama Veda)
- 4. Ayam Atma Brahma (अयम् आत्मा ब्रह्म) - "This Self is Brahman" (Mandukya Upanishad, Atharva Veda)

These Mahavakyas collectively express the ultimate truth of non-duality and the identity of the individual self with the supreme reality.

Let's try to understand a story from Chandogya Upanishad.

THE TALE OF UDDALAKA AND ŚVETAKETU: A JOURNEY TO "TAT TVAM ASI"

In the lush forests of ancient India, where the air was thick with the scent of sandalwood and the sound of Vedic chants echoed through the trees, there lived a renowned sage named Uddalaka Aruni. His ashram, a haven of learning and spiritual growth, was known far and wide for the wisdom that flowed from its hallowed grounds.

Uddalaka was not only a great teacher but also a father. His son, Śvetaketu, had just turned twelve, an age considered ripe for the commencement of formal education in the Vedic tradition. As Uddalaka gazed upon his son, he saw not just a child, but a vessel of immense potential, waiting to be filled with the nectar of knowledge.

One balmy morning, as the first rays of the sun painted the sky in hues of gold and crimson, Uddalaka called Śvetaketu to his side. The boy approached, his eyes wide with curiosity and anticipation.

"My son," Uddalaka began, his voice gentle yet firm, "you have reached the age of learning. It is time for you to embark on a journey of knowledge, to unravel the mysteries of our sacred texts, and to understand the nature of reality itself."

Śvetaketu's chest swelled with pride, expecting his father, the great sage, to take him under his wing. But Uddalaka had other plans.

"However," the sage continued, "the greatest lessons often come from beyond our familiar surroundings. Therefore, I have decided that you shall seek wisdom from another guru."

Confusion flickered across Śvetaketu's young face. "But father," he protested, "are you not the wisest of all? Why must I go elsewhere?"

Uddalaka smiled, his eyes twinkling with a mixture of affection and foresight. "There are truths, my dear Śvetaketu, that you must discover for yourself. Sometimes, to truly see, one must step away from the familiar. Go forth, learn from others, and return with not just knowledge, but wisdom."

And so, with a heart both heavy with separation and light with anticipation, Śvetaketu set out on his journey. He travelled to a distant ashram, renowned for its rigorous training in the Vedas and all associated branches of knowledge.

For twelve long years, Śvetaketu immersed himself in study. He pored over ancient texts, memorised countless verses, and engaged in passionate debates with his fellow students. He mastered the intricacies of Sanskrit grammar, delved deep into the Nyaya system of logic, explored the poetic depths of Kavya, and unravelled the mysteries of the Vedangas – the six auxiliary disciplines essential for Vedic study.

Days turned into weeks, weeks into months, and months into years. Śvetaketu's mind expanded, filled with knowledge like a river swelling in the monsoon rains. But as his intellect grew, so did his pride. He began to see himself as superior to his peers, believing that he had unravelled all the mysteries the world had to offer.

Finally, at the age of twenty-four, Śvetaketu completed his studies. His guru, impressed by his intellectual prowess, gave him his blessings and bid him return home. "Go, Śvetaketu," the teacher said, "and may your knowledge light the path for others."

With his head held high and his chest puffed with pride, Śvetaketu began the journey back to his father's ashram. He walked with the confident gait of one who believed he had conquered the realm of knowledge, ready to dazzle the world with his intellect.

As he approached the familiar grounds of his childhood home, Śvetaketu's heart raced with anticipation. He imagined the pride on his father's face, the admiration of the other disciples, the respect he would command with his vast learning.

Uddalaka, who had been anticipating his son's return, stood at the entrance of the ashram. His keen eyes took in the sight of his son – no longer a boy, but a man, carrying himself with the air of a scholar. But Uddalaka saw something else too, something that made his heart heavy – a veil of ignorance that still shrouded his son's understanding of the highest truth.

As Śvetaketu drew near, Uddalaka smiled warmly. "Welcome home, my son," he said, embracing Śvetaketu. "You have studied for twelve years and have gained much knowledge. Tell me, in all your learning, have you gained the understanding by which the unheard becomes heard, the unthought becomes thought, and the unknown becomes known?"

Śvetaketu's brow furrowed in confusion. He had expected praise, not questions. "What do you mean, father?" he asked, a hint of defensiveness in his voice. "I have studied all the Vedas, mastered grammar and logic. I can recite entire scriptures from memory. Surely I know all there is to know."

Uddalaka's eyes twinkled with a mixture of amusement and compassion. "Ah, but there is a knowledge beyond all you have learned, a truth that underlies all truths. Let me ask you this: have you learned that by knowing which, everything else becomes known?"

The young man's confidence wavered for the first time since his return. "I... I don't understand, father. How can knowing one thing lead to knowing everything?"

Uddalaka nodded, as if he had expected this response. "Come," he said, placing a gentle hand on his son's shoulder, "let us walk and talk. There are some things I must show you."

As they strolled through the ashram grounds, Uddalaka led Śvetaketu to a large banyan tree.

He plucked a small fruit from its branches and held it out to his son.

What do you see, Śvetaketu?" Uddalaka asked.

"A banyan fruit, of course," Śvetaketu replied, wondering where this was leading.

"Open it," Uddalaka instructed.

Śvetaketu did as he was told, revealing the tiny seeds within.

"Now, take one of these seeds and split it open," Uddalaka continued.

With some difficulty, Śvetaketu managed to split the tiny seed. "There's nothing inside, father," he said, peering closely at the halves of the seed.

Uddalaka smiled. "Ah, but there is, my son. That nothingness you see is the subtle essence from which this entire mighty banyan tree grows. That which you cannot see with your eyes is the power that creates all you can see. This subtle essence pervades the entire tree, giving it life and form. And just as this essence exists in the seed, there is an essence that pervades all of existence. That essence is the truth. That essence is the Self. And that, Śvetaketu, That thou art."

Śvetaketu listened, his mind grappling with this new perspective. But Uddalaka was not finished. He led his son to a nearby stream. Took a glass of water and asked Śvetaketu to add salt in it.

"Taste the water from the surface," Uddalaka said.

Śvetaketu did so. "It's salty," he reported.

"Now taste it from the middle."

Again, Śvetaketu tasted. "It's salty."

"Now from the bottom."

Once more, Śvetaketu tasted. "It's salty, father."

Uddalaka nodded, his eyes shining with the light of wisdom. "Just as you cannot see the salt, but can taste it throughout the water, so too is the eternal, infinite Brahman present throughout existence. You cannot see it with your eyes, but it is there, giving essence to all that exists. And that essence, my son, is not separate from you. That thou art – Tat Tvam Asi."

As the days passed, Uddalaka continued to guide Śvetaketu through various experiences and observations, each designed to illuminate the profound truth of "Tat Tvam Asi." He spoke of the essence in a banyan seed, invisible to the eye yet containing the potential for an entire tree. He demonstrated how salt, when dissolved in water, becomes unseen yet permeates the entire solution.

Gradually, Śvetaketu's initial arrogance gave way to a deep sense of wonder and humility. He began to see that true knowledge was not about accumulating information, but about realising a fundamental truth that transforms one's entire perception of reality.

The young man who had returned home full of pride in his learning now found himself on a new journey – one that led inward, to the very core of his being. He realised that all his years of study, while valuable, had only prepared him for this ultimate lesson.

Finally, after many such teachings, Uddalaka came to the central point of his instruction. "My dear Śvetaketu," he said, his eyes filled with compassion and love, "just as the salt pervades the water, unseen yet present in every part, so too does the eternal, infinite Brahman pervade all of existence. And here is the greatest truth of all – that essence, that ultimate reality, is not separate from you. Tat Tvam Asi – Thou Art That."

In that moment, something shifted in Śvetaketu's understanding. The veil of separation began to lift, and he glimpsed, if only for an instant, the profound unity underlying all things. He realised that his true self, the Atman, was not separate from Brahman, the ultimate reality. The years of study, the knowledge he had accumulated, all fell into place, illuminated by this single, radiant truth.

Śvetaketu fell at his father's feet, overwhelmed by the profundity of this realisation. "Father," he said, his voice trembling with emotion, "I see now that all my learning was but a preparation for this truth. I thought I knew everything, but I knew nothing of what truly matters. Please, teach me more."

Uddalaka helped his son to his feet and embraced him. "You have taken the first step on the true path of wisdom, my son. The journey of realising 'Tat Tvam Asi' is the work of a lifetime. But know this – in recognizing your own ignorance, you have gained the most important knowledge of all."

From that day forward, Śvetaketu approached his studies with a new humility and a deepened sense of purpose. He understood that true wisdom lay not in the accumulation of facts, but in the direct experience of the ultimate reality that underlies all existence.

And so, in the quiet of the ashram, under the patient guidance of his father, Śvetaketu continued his journey of self-discovery. The arrogant young scholar had transformed into a sincere seeker, his heart and mind opened to the profound truth of "Tat Tvam Asi" – Thou Art That.

As the story of Uddalaka and Śvetaketu spread, it became a beacon for seekers of truth across the land. It reminded all who heard it that the greatest wisdom often comes not from books or lectures, but from the patient guidance of a true teacher and the sincere openness of a devoted student. And most importantly, it carried the timeless message that the divine essence we seek is not distant or separate, but is our very own true nature – Tat Tvam Asi.

Reflection

The teaching of "Tat Tvam Asi" invites us to transcend the illusion of separateness and recognize our unity with the cosmos. Through the story of Uddalaka and Śvetaketu, we gain insight into the deep interconnectedness of all existence. By understanding and internalising this truth, we move closer to the ultimate realisation of our true nature as one with Brahman.

This chapter sets the foundation for exploring the deep spiritual wisdom of the Upanishads, guiding us towards a greater understanding of our place in the universe and the essence of our being.

THE SEEKER'S DILEMMA: NACHIKETA AND YAMA

Imagine standing at the threshold of death itself, face to face with the lord of the Death. What would you ask for? Wealth beyond measure? The power to control life and death? Or would you have the courage to seek something far more valuable - the knowledge of what lies beyond life?

This is not merely a hypothetical scenario, but the heart of one of the most profound stories in Hindu philosophy - the tale of Nachiketa and Yama from the Katha Upanishad.

The Sacrifice and a Father's Anger

Our story begins in ancient India, in the household of a sage named Vājashravas. Known for his piety and adherence to religious duties,Vājashravas decided to perform a great sacrifice known as Vishwajit, with the hope of attaining heavenly rewards. As part of this sacrifice, he was required to give away all his possessions.

However, Vājashrava's son, the young and perceptive Nachiketa, observed something troubling. His father was not giving away his best possessions but instead offering old, weak, and barren cows. Nachiketa, though young, understood the importance of sincerity in religious rituals. He thought to himself, "Surely, these offerings of little value will not lead to heaven."

Driven by a combination of youthful idealism and a deep sense of dharma (righteous duty), Nachiketa approached his father. With innocence and courage, he asked, "Father, to whom will you offer me?"

Vājashravas, busy with the intricacies of the sacrifice, ignored his son's question. But Nachiketa, persistent in his quest for truth and proper conduct, repeated his question three times. Irritated by the interruption and perhaps stung by the implicit criticism of his actions, Vajashravasa responded in anger, **"I give you to Death (Yama)!"**

The moment these words left Vājashrava's lips, a profound silence fell over the sacrificial grounds. Both father and son realised the gravity of what had been said. In the culture of ancient India, a father's words, especially during a sacred ritual, carried the weight of an irrevocable vow.

Nachiketa's Journey to the Realm of Death

Nachiketa, displaying wisdom and courage beyond his years, decided to honour his father's words. He said, "Father, your word is your bond. I shall go to the house of Death." In this moment, Nachiketa demonstrated not only his respect for his father and the sanctity of the spoken word but also his fearlessness in the face of death itself.

And so, the young Nachiketa set out on his journey to the realm of Yama, the god of death. As he travelled, he contemplated the nature of death, the meaning of life, and the purpose of existence - questions that have haunted humanity since time immemorial.

Upon reaching Yama's abode, Nachiketa found it empty. The lord of death was away, and Nachiketa waited patiently for three days and nights without food or water. This period of waiting, a test of sorts, symbolises the perseverance and dedication required on the spiritual path.

Yama's Return and the Three Boons

When Yama returned and found that a Brahmin boy had been waiting at his doorstep without hospitality for three nights, he was deeply troubled. In the Hindu tradition, failing to provide hospitality to a guest, especially a Brahmin, was considered a grave sin. To make amends, Yama offered Nachiketa three boons - three wishes that he would fulfil.

For his first boon, Nachiketa, showing his compassion and devotion to his father, asked: "Let my father's anger be appeased, let him recognize me when I return, and let him greet me with love." This wish reveals Nachiketa's lack of resentment towards his father and his desire for familial harmony.

Yama granted this wish readily, impressed by the boy's forgiveness and filial piety.

For his second boon, Nachiketa requested knowledge of the fire sacrifice that leads to heaven. He said, "Teach me the fire sacrifice that leads to heaven, for I know that those who perform it correctly attain immortality and bliss."

Yama, pleased with Nachiketa's interest in spiritual matters, granted this wish too, imparting to him the sacred knowledge of the fire ritual. He even declared that this fire sacrifice would henceforth be known as the "Nachiketa Fire."

It was Nachiketa's third wish, however, that would form the crux of this profound philosophical discourse. Nachiketa asked, "There is this doubt about a man when he dies. Some say he exists, others say he does not. I want to know the truth. Please teach me about this ultimate secret - what happens after death?"

Yama, the god of death himself, was taken aback by this request. He tried to dissuade Nachiketa, offering him instead long life, wealth, earthly pleasures, and even lordship over vast realms. "Ask for sons and grandsons who shall live a hundred years. Ask for a lot of cattle, elephants, gold, and horses. Ask for vast expanses of land, and live yourself as many years as you desire," Yama tempted.

But Nachiketa, displaying wisdom far beyond his years, remained steadfast. He replied, "These things are transient. They wear out the vigour of all the senses. Even the longest life is short indeed. Keep your horses and let me know the truth

Nachiketa's response encapsulates one of the core teachings of Hindu philosophy - the ephemeral nature of material pleasures and the superiority of spiritual knowledge. He continued, "How can these be enjoyed by one who knows of their fleeting nature? Tell me only of the great hereafter. This is the only boon I choose."

Yama, deeply impressed by Nachiketa's discernment and unwavering focus on the highest truth, realised that he had found a worthy student. He said, "I will tell you this secret, for you have turned away from the temptation of wealth and the longest span of life. Before you, many have failed to comprehend this subtle truth."

The Great Teaching: Atman and Brahman

What followed was a profound discourse on the nature of the self (Atman) and its relationship to the ultimate reality (Brahman). Yama began by explaining the sacred syllable Om, describing it as the imperishable Brahman, the highest end to which all spiritual aspirants strive.

He then delved into the nature of the Atman, the eternal self that exists beyond the body and mind. "The Self," Yama explained, "is not born, nor does it die. It did not spring from anything, nor did anything spring from it. Unborn, eternal, everlasting, and ancient, it is not slain when the body is slain."

Yama continued, drawing analogies to help Nachiketa understand this subtle concept. He compared the Atman to a rider in a chariot, with the body as the chariot, the intellect as the charioteer, and the mind as the reins. The senses, he said, were like the horses, and the objects of the senses were the paths they travelled.

"One who has no understanding and whose mind is never firmly held, his senses are uncontrolled, like vicious horses of a charioteer," Yama cautioned. "But one who has understanding and whose mind is always firmly held, his senses are under control, like good horses of a charioteer."

Through these teachings, Yama was guiding Nachiketa towards the realisation that true immortality lies not in extending physical life indefinitely, but in realising one's identity with the eternal, unchanging Atman.

The Path to Self-Realisation

Yama then outlined the path to self-realisation, emphasising the importance of discrimination, detachment, and concentration. He taught Nachiketa about the hierarchy of spiritual evolution: "Higher than the senses are the objects of sense. Higher than the objects of sense is the mind. Higher than the mind is the intellect.

Higher than the intellect is the great Atman. Higher than the great Atman is the Unmanifested. Higher than the Unmanifested is the Person. Higher than the Person there is nothing at all. That is the end, that is the highest goal."

He stressed the difficulty of this path, saying, "Sharp as a razor's edge, hard to traverse, difficult to tread is this path, say the sages." Yet, he assured Nachiketa that one who has realised the Self through inner tranquillity and self-control goes beyond sorrow.

Yama concluded his teaching with a powerful statement on the nature of liberation: "When all the knots of the heart are cut asunder here on earth, then a mortal becomes immortal. This much alone is the teaching."

Nachiketa's Enlightenment and Return

Having received this profound knowledge directly from the god of death, Nachiketa attained enlightenment. He had gained not just an intellectual understanding, but a direct realisation of the eternal nature of the Self.

Yama, pleased with his student's comprehension and realisation, gave Nachiketa one final boon. He declared that the fire sacrifice would henceforth be known by Nachiketa's name, and that anyone who performed this sacrifice three times would be liberated from the cycle of birth and death.

With this knowledge and these gifts, Nachiketa returned to the world of the living. He was greeted by his father with love and recognition, fulfilling the first boon he had asked of Yama. Nachiketa lived the rest of his life spreading the wisdom he had gained, helping others on the path to self-realisation.

Reflection

The story of Nachiketa and Yama highlights the value of seeking deeper truths beyond the ephemeral pleasures of the material world. It underscores the importance of questioning, learning, and understanding the true nature of the self. Nachiketa's unwavering pursuit of knowledge and Yama's revelations provide a powerful lesson on the quest for spiritual wisdom and the realisation of the eternal self.

This chapter serves as a compelling exploration of the Upanishadic teaching that true fulfilment comes from understanding the nature of existence and recognizing the eternal essence within us all.

The story of Nachiketa and Yama, while ancient, continues to resonate with spiritual seekers today. It teaches us several timeless lessons:

1. The courage to face our deepest fears, symbolised by Nachiketa's willingness to confront death itself.
2. The discernment to recognize the transient nature of material pleasures and the supreme value of spiritual knowledge.
3. The persistence required on the spiritual path, as exemplified by Nachiketa's unwavering focus on the highest truth despite temptations.
4. The profound non-dual philosophy of Advaita Vedanta, which asserts the ultimate unity of the individual self (Atman) with the universal Self (Brahman).
5. The importance of finding a worthy teacher (guru) who can impart true knowledge.

In a world often driven by material pursuits and fleeting pleasures, Nachiketa's story serves as a powerful reminder of what truly matters. It encourages us to look beyond the superficial, to question deeply, and to seek the eternal amidst the ephemeral.

SAGE VAMADEVA'S REALISATION OF THE SELF AS BRAHMAN: REALISING SELF AS BRAHAMAN

The Aitareya Upanishad presents one of the earliest accounts of self-realisation through the story of Sage Vamadeva. The essence of this story is the core Upanishadic teaching that the individual self (Atman) is identical with the universal reality (Brahman). This knowledge, once realised, leads to liberation (moksha), freeing one from the cycle of birth and death.

The Story: Vamadeva's Enlightenment

Sage Vamadeva's journey toward self-realisation is unique because it is said to have occurred while he was still in the womb. The Aitareya Upanishad tells us that Vamadeva, even before his birth, attained a profound understanding of the ultimate truth—that his individual self was not separate from the universal consciousness.

Vamadeva's mother was carrying him, and as he lay within her womb, he reflected upon the nature of his existence. Even in this limited physical state, he was not distracted by the material limitations of his body. Instead, he was able to reach beyond the physical, perceiving the underlying unity of existence.

As his awareness grew, Vamadeva began to realise that the same force which animated his own being also pervaded the entire universe. He perceived the life force that connected all living beings and saw himself not as a mere individual, but as one with the very essence of creation.

In a moment of profound insight, Vamadeva declared, "I, Vamadeva, knew all the births of the gods." This statement is rich with meaning. By saying he "knew all the births of the gods," Vamadeva was expressing his understanding that the divine essence—the same essence that manifests in the gods—was present within him. He saw beyond the apparent multiplicity of forms and recognized the singular reality that binds everything together. He realised that Atman, his true self, was Brahman—the infinite and eternal consciousness that underlies all existence.

This realisation transformed Vamadeva. He was no longer bound by the ignorance that causes human beings to see themselves as separate from the rest of the universe. He understood that birth and death were mere illusions; his true self was beyond these, eternal and changeless. This was the realisation of the ultimate truth—Tat Tvam Asi—that the individual self is one with the universal self.

The Significance of Vamadeva's Story

Vamadeva's story is remarkable because it demonstrates that the realisation of one's unity with Brahman can occur even in the most unlikely of circumstances, such as while still in the womb. This teaches that the potential for enlightenment is present within each of us, regardless of the external conditions. What is required is the deep insight to see beyond the illusions of the material world.

The Aitareya Upanishad does not elaborate on Vamadeva's life after this realisation, but the importance of his story lies in the profound wisdom he attained. This knowledge freed him from the cycle of birth and death, granting him liberation (moksha).

The Upanishadic sages understood that liberation is not a result of external actions or rituals but comes from inner realisation— understanding the true nature of the self as

Brahman. The story of Vamadeva serves as a powerful reminder that such knowledge can be attained by anyone who seeks it with sincerity and dedication.

1. Innate Wisdom: The story suggests that the highest spiritual wisdom is not something external to be acquired, but an innate truth waiting to be realised. Vamadeva's prenatal enlightenment symbolises the potential for self-realisation that exists within each of us from the very beginning.

2. Transcendence of Physical Limitations: By attaining enlightenment while still in the womb, Vamadeva demonstrates that true realisation is not dependent on physical maturity or external circumstances. It is a state of consciousness that transcends bodily limitations.

3. Unity of Atman and Brahman: The core teaching of the Upanishads - the identity of the individual self (Atman) with the universal self (Brahman) - is vividly illustrated in

Vamadeva's experience. His declaration of knowing "all the births of these Devas" indicates his recognition of the one consciousness underlying all manifestations.

4. Liberation from Samsara: Vamadeva's realisation freed him from the cycle of birth and death (samsara). This underscores the Upanishadic teaching that true knowledge (jnana) is the key to liberation (moksha).

5. Symbolism of the Hawk: The metaphor of flying forth "like a hawk" represents the swift and direct nature of self-realisation. Once the truth is perceived, the liberation is immediate and complete.

6. Challenge to Conventional Wisdom: The story challenges conventional notions about the nature of consciousness and the process of spiritual awakening. It suggests that enlightenment is not the result of a long process of learning and practice, but can be a sudden, direct insight into one's true nature.

7. Inspiration for Seekers: For spiritual aspirants, Vamadeva's story serves as

an inspiration, reminding them that the highest truth is always present and can be realised at any moment, if one can see beyond the veils of illusion.

"SARVAM KHALVIDAM BRAHMA" (ALL THIS IS BRAHMAN)

The teaching of "Sarvam Khalvidam Brahma" appears in the **Chandogya Upanishad (3.14.1)** and translates to "All this is Brahman." It conveys the idea that everything in the universe—every object, every being, and every phenomenon—is a manifestation of the ultimate reality, Brahman. This principle emphasises that Brahman is not distant or separate from the world, but rather is the essence that permeates all of existence.

This realisation challenges the dualistic view of the universe, where things seem separate and distinct. Instead, it encourages the seeker to see the oneness of everything in the cosmos, understanding that all diversity is an expression of a singular, infinite consciousness.

The Story: Indra and Virochana's Quest for Brahman

In ancient times, two prominent figures—**Indra**, the king of the gods, and **Virochana**, the king of the demons—set out on a journey to uncover the nature of Brahman, the ultimate reality. Both were motivated by the desire for wisdom, and their teacher was none other than **Prajapati**, the lord of creation. However, while they both sought knowledge, their motives and understandings would lead them to very different conclusions.

Indra and Virochana approached Prajapati with reverence, requesting to be taught the nature of Brahman. Prajapati agreed but imposed a condition: they must live with him as students for 32 years. After years of dedication and service, Prajapati was satisfied with their commitment and began the first stage of their instruction.

Prajapati told them, "The self that is seen in the eyes or in a reflection—that is Brahman." Upon hearing this, both Indra and Virochana believed they had understood the nature of Brahman. They looked into a mirror, saw their own physical reflections, and concluded that the body itself must be Brahman. Delighted, they thought the quest was complete, and Virochana left to return to the world of the demons, convinced that the body was the ultimate reality.

Indra, however, on his journey back, began to have doubts. He realised that if the body were Brahman, then Brahman would be subject to ageing, decay, and death. How could Brahman, the eternal and unchanging reality, be something as transient as the physical body?

With these doubts gnawing at him, Indra returned to Prajapati and confessed his uncertainty. Prajapati smiled and told him that his questioning spirit had put him on the right path, but there was more to learn. Indra stayed for another period of study, during which Prajapati offered deeper insights.

Prajapati next taught Indra that Brahman was not the physical body but rather the inner self experienced in dreams. Indra once again thought he had understood, believing that the self in dreams must be Brahman. But as he reflected more, he realised that even in dreams, the self is subject to illusions and distortions—it is not free from the limitations of the mind.

Indra, unsatisfied with this partial understanding, returned to Prajapati for further guidance. Again, Prajapati explained that Indra had progressed but had yet to grasp the full truth. Over several more stages of instruction, Prajapati revealed that Brahman is neither the body nor the mind, nor even the self experienced in dreams or deep sleep. Instead, Brahman is the pure consciousness that underlies and transcends all states of being.

In the end, Indra realised that Brahman is the ultimate, formless reality that pervades everything. It is not limited by physical or mental conditions. This truth—that Brahman is all-encompassing, beyond any singular form or state—brought Indra to enlightenment. He understood the profound teaching of "Sarvam Khalvidam Brahma"—that **everything in the universe, from the highest god to the smallest creature, is a manifestation of Brahman**.

Meanwhile, Virochana, having misunderstood the teaching, returned to the demons and propagated the false idea that the body is the self. He led his followers to believe that bodily pleasures and material satisfaction were the ultimate goals of life, a philosophy that kept them trapped in ignorance and illusion.

Reflection: The True Nature of Brahman

The contrasting journeys of Indra and Virochana reflect the two possible paths in the quest for self-realisation: one that leads to true wisdom, and one that leads to misunderstanding and ignorance. Indra's willingness to question and seek deeper truth allowed him to see beyond the physical and mental layers of existence, ultimately realising the all-pervading nature of Brahman.

The story teaches that true wisdom comes from recognizing the oneness of all things. While the world appears to be full of distinctions and separations—between self and other, life and death, material and spiritual—these are all manifestations of the same underlying reality, Brahman. **Indra's enlightenment reveals that understanding the universe's essential unity is key to liberation** from ignorance and suffering.

Virochana's failure to grasp this truth illustrates the danger of stopping at superficial understandings. By equating Brahman with the body, he remained trapped in the illusions of material existence, unable to see the eternal essence beyond.

Conclusion

"Sarvam Khalvidam Brahma" calls us to expand our vision of the universe and ourselves. It asks us to look beyond appearances and recognize the unity of all things, to understand that every being and every object is a manifestation of the same cosmic reality. The story of Indra and Virochana reminds us that true knowledge comes from persistent inquiry and a willingness to look beyond the obvious, for only then can we see the infinite Brahman that permeates everything.

THE STORY OF THE COSMIC EGG (HIRANYAGARBHA)

Have you ever gazed at the night sky and wondered about the origins of our vast universe? How did everything we know come into existence? These questions have captivated human minds for millennia, spawning countless myths, theories, and philosophical inquiries. Today, we embark on a journey through time and space to explore an ancient story that attempts to answer these profound questions - the tale of the Cosmic Egg, known in Hindu tradition as Hiranyagarbha.

In the beginning, there was nothing. No sky, no earth, no light, no sound—only the endless expanse of the formless Brahman, an infinite consciousness, silent and still. Out of this profound stillness, something remarkable began to take shape. A single point of golden light appeared, shimmering in the void. Slowly, it expanded, taking on the form of a radiant egg. This was no ordinary egg; it was Hiranyagarbha, the golden womb, containing within it the seed of all existence.

Inside this cosmic egg, all the elements of creation lay dormant, waiting to be born. The first stirrings of life began within its glowing shell. The potential for everything—the stars, the planets, the oceans, and even life itself—was enclosed in this divine womb. Then, with a mighty breath, the egg split open, and from it, the universe spilled forth in a magnificent display of creation.

As the shell of Hiranyagarbha cracked open, it released the five fundamental elements—earth, water, fire, air, and ether. These elements combined and separated, forming the structures of the cosmos. The sky was lifted high, the oceans filled their depths, and the earth found its place in the vastness of space. Time and space, once formless, now had meaning and boundaries. Light and dark, day and night, rhythm and order emerged from the primal chaos.

At the heart of this creation was Brahman, the ultimate reality, who did not create the universe as an external being but as an inherent force that permeated every aspect of existence. Hiranyagarbha was both the seed and the vessel of creation, a manifestation of Brahman's limitless potential. Brahman's essence flowed through everything—the planets, the stars, the oceans, and even the smallest creatures. Every soul, every being, was a part of this cosmic process, connected through the eternal presence of Brahman.

This cosmic egg story is not just a myth; it is a profound teaching on the nature of existence. It reveals that everything in the universe, from the vast galaxies to the smallest atom, originates from the same source. We, too, carry within us the essence of Brahman, the same creative force that birthed the universe.

To understand the significance of the Cosmic Egg, we must first grasp the fundamental concept of Brahman in Hindu philosophy. Brahman is the ultimate reality, the formless, infinite, and eternal essence that underlies all of existence. It is from this boundless source that the universe, with all its diversity and complexity, is said to have sprung forth.

The Cosmic Egg serves as a powerful symbol in Hindu cosmology, representing the transition from the formless Brahman to the manifest universe. It encapsulates the idea that all of creation, in its infinite variety, emerged from a single source - a concept that resonates with modern scientific theories about the origin of the universe.

From the golden egg, the basic elements of the universe come into being as

1. Akasha (Ether): The subtle, all-pervading field that serves as the medium for all phenomena.
2. Vayu (Air): The principle of movement and the breath of life.
3. Agni (Fire): The energy that transforms and illuminates.
4. Jala (Water): The fluid principle that adapts and nurtures.
5. Prithvi (Earth): The solid foundation that provides stability and form.

These five elements, known as the Pancha Mahabhuta, form the building blocks of all material existence. Their various combinations and interactions give rise to the infinite diversity we see in the world around us.

As the elements take shape, so too do the fundamental aspects of existence:

- Time (Kala) emerges, bringing with it the concepts of past, present, and future.
- Space (Akasha) unfolds, providing the stage upon which the cosmic drama will play out.
- Consciousness (Chit) awakens, imbuing the universe with awareness and the potential for life.

Brahman as the Ultimate Source

While the story of Hiranyagarbha describes a process of creation, it's crucial to understand that in Hindu philosophy, Brahman remains the ultimate source and substance of all that exists. The Cosmic Egg and its contents are not separate from Brahman but are manifestations of its infinite potential.

This concept is beautifully expressed in the Chandogya Upanishad, which states: "In the beginning was only Being, One without a second. Out of itself, it created the universe." This profound statement encapsulates the non-dual nature of reality in Hindu thought.

The individual soul, or Atman, is seen as a spark of the universal soul, Brahman. Just as a wave is not separate from the ocean but a temporary expression of it, so too is each individual consciousness a manifestation of the universal consciousness.

In this view, creation is not a one-time event but a cyclical process. The universe emerges from Brahman, exists for a cosmic cycle (known as a Kalpa), and then dissolves back into Brahman, only to emerge again in an eternal cycle of creation and dissolution.

Reflection and Meaning

The story of the Cosmic Egg is rich with symbolism and philosophical insights that remain relevant to our modern understanding of the world:

- **Order from Chaos**: The emergence of the structured universe from the formless Brahman mirrors the scientific concept of complexity arising from simplicity, as seen in theories like the Big Bang.
- **Unity in Diversity**: Just as all aspects of the universe emerge from a single source in the myth, modern physics suggests that all matter and energy in the universe were once unified in a singularity.
- **Microcosm and Macrocosm**: The idea that the individual (microcosm) reflects the nature of the universe (macrocosm) is a recurring theme in many philosophical and spiritual traditions. It suggests a deep interconnectedness between all aspects of existence.
- **Potential and Manifestation**: The Cosmic Egg represents the transition from potential to actuality, a process that we see

reflected in our own lives as we grow, learn, and realise our inherent capabilities.

- **Cycles of Renewal:** The cyclical nature of creation and dissolution in Hindu cosmology reminds us of the constant renewal and transformation in our own lives and in the natural world around us.

The story of Hiranyagarbha, the Cosmic Egg, offers us a profound metaphor for understanding our place in the universe. It suggests that we are not separate from the world around us but are integral parts of a grand, interconnected whole.

As we reflect on this ancient tale, we are invited to consider our own origins and our connection to the vast cosmos. Are we not, in a sense, cosmic eggs ourselves - containing within us the potential for great creativity, transformation, and realisation?

The next time you gaze at the night sky, remember the story of the Cosmic Egg. Let it remind you of the wonder and mystery of existence, and of your own role in the ongoing story of the universe. For in understanding the origins of all things, we may come to better understand ourselves.

"SATYAMEVA JAYATE" (TRUTH ALONE TRIUMPHS)

In a distant time, in the land of Ayodhya, there lived a king named Harishchandra. Renowned for his sense of justice and virtue, Harishchandra ruled his kingdom with fairness, compassion, and integrity. Under his rule, Ayodhya flourished, and his subjects loved him for his unwavering commitment to dharma, or righteous conduct. But beyond his duties as a king, Harishchandra held one principle above all others: truth, or Satya. He believed that truth was the highest form of dharma, and that in the end, truth would always triumph.

However, the greatness of King Harishchandra was to be tested by the gods themselves. One day, the great sage Vishwamitra appeared before the king, his face stern yet majestic. He had come to test Harishchandra's commitment to truth. In a calm voice, Vishwamitra asked the king to fulfil a promise he had made in a past life—a promise that the king had no memory of but which bound him to give up his entire kingdom.

Harishchandra, being true to his word, did not hesitate. With a heavy heart, he relinquished his throne, his palace, and his wealth to the sage. He, his wife Shaivya, and their young son Rohitashva left the kingdom in exile, carrying nothing with them except their clothes and their commitment to truth.

The Test of Truth

Their troubles, however, had only begun. As Harishchandra wandered the forests, his family, once surrounded by the luxuries of royal life, now faced the harsh realities of hunger and poverty. Yet even in these dire circumstances, the king refused to compromise his principles. His wife, Shaivya, pleaded with him to reconsider his strict adherence to the truth, to bend just once, to lie if it meant they could reclaim their lives. But Harishchandra stood firm. He believed that abandoning truth for temporary relief would be a far greater loss than any material suffering they endured.

But fate was not done testing him. Vishwamitra, determined to push Harishchandra to the edge, imposed another condition. To complete the sage's demands, Harishchandra needed to pay dakshina (an offering) to the sage, a sum of money that was impossible for the exiled king to afford. In desperation, Harishchandra sold himself into slavery, offering his service to a cruel cremation ground keeper. He took up the grim task of preparing bodies for their final rites—a far cry from his days as a king, but he accepted his fate as a servant of truth.

The Struggle and Sacrifice

Time passed, and the trials of King Harishchandra only grew heavier. His wife, Shaivya, found work as a servant, while their son Rohitashva grew weak from the struggles of their new life. Then came the darkest hour. Rohitashva, the only child of Harishchandra, fell gravely ill and died. Devastated, Shaivya carried her son's body to the cremation ground where her husband worked, but she had no money to pay for the cremation rites.

Harishchandra, now the keeper of the cremation grounds, was torn apart by the gravity of the situation. As his wife sobbed before him, begging for mercy, he still refused to break his oath. "How can I abandon my duty, even now?" he thought. "If I let emotion sway me, I betray the truth itself."

Shaivya, shattered by grief, was prepared to endure her husband's decision. In his heart, Harishchandra wept, but he did not waver. He prepared to perform the rites, knowing that he could not accept his own son's body without proper payment. It was then, at the peak of his suffering, that divine intervention occurred.

The Triumph of Truth

Moved by the king's unbreakable commitment to truth, the gods themselves descended. Vishwamitra, along with the other gods, revealed themselves and praised Harishchandra for his steadfastness. All his trials had been a divine test, and he had passed. His son was miraculously revived, his kingdom was restored, and the king was honoured by the gods for his unwavering dedication to truth.

Harishchandra's suffering had not been in vain. He had shown that truth, even when it brings hardship and sorrow, ultimately leads to victory. "Satyameva Jayate"—Truth Alone Triumphs— became the immortal legacy of Harishchandra's story. He returned to Ayodhya, his head held high, not because of the wealth or power he regained, but because he had remained true to his principles.

Reflection and Teachings of "Satyameva Jayate

The story of King Harishchandra resonates deeply with the teachings of the Upanishads. It is not just a story of personal sacrifice; it is a reminder of the profound connection between truth and liberation. By holding fast to the principle of satya, Harishchandra showed that truth is not merely a moral choice—it is the very essence of the path to moksha, or spiritual freedom.

Harishchandra's journey illustrates that truth may not always bring immediate rewards. In fact, it may lead to suffering, loss, and despair. But in the end, truth is its own reward, for it is the only thing that can bring lasting peace and liberation. The material world is transient, filled with illusions and falsehoods, but truth is eternal. By aligning oneself with truth, one aligns with the very nature of Brahman, the ultimate reality.

In our own lives, we are often tempted to abandon truth for convenience, comfort, or gain. The story of Harishchandra challenges us to reflect on the role of truth in our own journey. Are we willing to sacrifice temporary pleasures for the sake of truth? Do we have the courage to stand by our principles, even when faced with hardship? The story of Harishchandra teaches us that truth is not just a principle to be followed when it is easy, but a path that must be walked, no matter the cost.

THE STORY OF SAGE YAJNAVALKYA

In the peaceful forests of ancient India, there lived a wise and celebrated sage named Yajnavalkya. His wisdom was sought by kings and commoners alike, for Yajnavalkya was known not only for his knowledge of the Vedas but for his deep understanding of the ultimate truths of existence. He was a man who had realised the impermanence of worldly life and sought only one thing: the knowledge of the self, the Atman.

Yajnavalkya lived with his two wives, Maitreyi and Katyayani. While Katyayani was content with the comforts of family life, Maitreyi was different. She was a seeker of truth, drawn to the deeper questions of existence. One day, Yajnavalkya decided that the time had come for him to renounce his household life and pursue the final stage of life—sannyasa, the path of renunciation.

He gathered his wives and told them of his decision. "I am going to renounce the world and leave behind all my possessions," Yajnavalkya said. "I will divide my wealth between you both."

Katyayani accepted the offer without question, for she valued the material security it would bring. But Maitreyi, with her mind always on higher pursuits, asked a question that would lead to one of the most profound teachings in the Upanishads.

The Wisdom of Maitreyi

Maitreyi, wise beyond her years, looked at her husband and asked, "Yajnavalkya, if I were to possess all the wealth in the world, would it bring me immortality? Would it help me achieve eternal happiness?"

Yajnavalkya paused, his eyes filled with admiration for her insight. "No," he replied. "Wealth cannot bring immortality. In fact, it can only give you a fleeting sense of happiness, bound by the limitations of the material world."

Maitreyi, uninterested in the temporary pleasures that wealth could provide, responded, "Then what use is wealth to me? Teach me what you know. Teach me about the Atman, the self, so that I may attain true knowledge and liberation."

Yajnavalkya smiled, recognizing the depth of her spiritual thirst. He realised that Maitreyi was ready to learn the ultimate truth, one that transcended worldly possessions and the temporary joys they offered. So he began to teach her the nature of the Atman, the essence of all beings.

Yajnavalkya's Teachings on the Atman

Yajnavalkya spoke to Maitreyi with a calm voice, as if unveiling the secrets of the universe itself. "Maitreyi," he said, "it is not for the sake of wealth, nor for the sake of possessions, that people seek happiness. They desire these things for the sake of the self. It is the self, the Atman, that is the source of all love and joy. It is because the self resides within us that we seek fulfilment in the world. But the world, with all its pleasures and pains, cannot satisfy the deepest longing of the heart, for it is impermanent."

He continued, "The Atman is beyond birth and death. It is eternal, untouched by the transient nature of the material world. Everything else—wealth, fame, relationships—comes and goes. But the Atman remains. To realise this self is to realise the essence of Brahman, the ultimate reality. Only by knowing the self can one attain immortality and true happiness."

Maitreyi listened intently, her mind absorbing the profound wisdom her husband shared. She began to see that the pursuit of external wealth and success was only a distraction from the real goal of life: the realisation of the self.

-Renunciation and the Path to Liberation

As Yajnavalkya prepared to leave his household life, he made it clear that renunciation was not about abandoning the world, but about transcending it. "To renounce the world," he explained, "is not to reject life, but to see life for what it truly is—a play of impermanent forms. Renunciation allows us to detach from illusions and attachments so that we can focus on what is eternal: the Atman."

Yajnavalkya's path was not one of withdrawal from responsibility, but of moving beyond the ego's desires. He had mastered the art of living without attachment, knowing that the true self, the Atman, is not bound by the material or emotional circumstances of the world. By renouncing his wealth and his position, Yajnavalkya sought to dwell in the ultimate reality, free from the distractions of worldly life.

His teachings to Maitreyi were not just philosophical musings, but a guide to liberation. He taught her that knowledge of the Atman was the key to moksha, the ultimate release from the cycle of birth and death. "Those who realise the self," he said, "transcend the world of appearances and enter the realm of truth."

Reflection and Spiritual Significance

The story of Yajnavalkya and Maitreyi speaks to the heart of spiritual seekers across generations. It challenges us to reflect on our own lives, to ask whether we are chasing temporary joys or seeking the eternal truth of the self. Yajnavalkya's teachings remind us that the material world, though alluring, is ultimately impermanent. The wealth and success we strive for will one day fade away, but the knowledge of the self endures.

Maitreyi's wisdom is a beacon for those who prioritise knowledge and self-realisation over material gain. Her desire to learn the truth of the Atman teaches us that true fulfilment comes not from external possessions, but from understanding our inner nature.

In today's fast-paced world, where success is often measured by wealth and status, the story of Yajnavalkya offers a counter-narrative. It tells us that wisdom, not wealth, is the key to lasting peace. It encourages us to look inward, to question the value we place on external achievements, and to seek the truth that lies within.

Sage Yajnavalkya's teachings are a timeless reminder of the wisdom of renunciation and self-knowledge. In his dialogue with Maitreyi, he reveals the impermanence of worldly possessions and the enduring nature of the self. He teaches us that true happiness does not come from wealth or success, but from realising the Atman, the essence of all beings.

As we navigate our own journeys, may we learn from the wisdom of Yajnavalkya. May we seek knowledge over material gain, and may we remember that the ultimate path to liberation lies within, in the discovery of the eternal self.

THE FORBIDDEN FRUIT OF LUST: THE STORY OF BHARTHARI AND PINGALA

In ancient India, there was a powerful king named Bharthari, known for his bravery, wisdom, and devotion to his kingdom. Yet despite his many achievements, he had one weakness—his deep and consuming love for his queen, Pingala. Bharthari was infatuated with her beauty and charm, and his love for her blinded him to her faults.

One day, a great sage visited the king and offered him a magical fruit, which, he said, had the power to grant immortality and eternal youth. "This fruit is a gift for someone you love," said the sage. Bharthari, overwhelmed with love for Pingala, decided that she, above all others, deserved this gift. He presented the fruit to Pingala, hoping to show her the depth of his affection and trust.

Pingala's Betrayal

However, Pingala's heart did not belong solely to Bharthari. Unknown to the king, she was involved in an affair with a paramour—a man with whom she shared an illicit bond of passion. When Bharthari gave her the fruit, instead of treasuring it, she chose to give it to her lover. "He deserves this more than the king," she thought, convinced that her love for him was more real and intense than her obligations to Bharthari.

Pingala handed the fruit to her paramour, believing it would bring them closer. But her lover, who had his own desires and loyalties, saw no value in keeping it. Instead, he passed the fruit to his own secret lover, thinking she deserved it more. This cycle of betrayal continued, with the fruit moving from one pair of hands to another, each time reflecting the treacherous nature of lust and deception.

The Fruit's Journey

The fruit, which had once been a symbol of Bharthari's love, was now caught in a web of lies and betrayal. It journeyed through a series of hands, moving from Pingala's paramour to his lover, and then on to yet another. Finally, in a cruel twist of fate, the fruit made its way back to Bharthari. The very gift he had given out of love now returned to him, tainted by the deceit of those around him.

When Bharthari realised what had happened—that the fruit had been passed from one unfaithful lover to another, only to return to him—his heart shattered. He was overcome with sorrow, not just for Pingala's betrayal, but for the realisation that everything he had placed his trust in—his love, his desires, and his attachments—was fleeting and unreliable.

This moment of profound disillusionment marked a turning point in Bharthari's life. He understood, for the first time, the impermanence of worldly pleasures and the dangers of attachment to lust and desire. His love for Pingala, which had once seemed so pure and real, was revealed to be nothing more than a fleeting illusion, driven by passion rather than truth.

Bharthari's sorrow soon gave way to a deeper understanding. He realised that as long as one is attached to desires—whether for love, wealth, or power—one will be trapped in a cycle of suffering. Lust, he saw, was like the fruit that had passed through so many hands—always promising fulfilment but never delivering true satisfaction.

Bharthari's Renunciation

With this new wisdom, Bharthari made a life-altering decision. He renounced the world, leaving behind his kingdom, his wealth, and even his beloved Pingala. He chose to walk away from the illusions that had once captivated him and sought the deeper truths of life. Bharthari retreated into the forest, where he became a wandering ascetic, dedicating himself to the pursuit of spiritual knowledge.

During his time in the wilderness, Bharthari wrote the **Niti Shataka**, a collection of a hundred verses that reflected his newfound wisdom. These verses spoke of the transient nature of worldly desires, the futility of chasing after material pleasures, and the importance of cultivating wisdom and self-restraint. In the "Niti Satakam," Bharthari shared the lessons he had learned from his own experiences, warning others not to be blinded by lust, greed, or attachment.

Reflection and Key Takeaways

Bharthari's story offers several important lessons that resonate deeply with the teachings of the Upanishads. The first lesson is the **danger of lust**. Lust, like any strong desire, can cloud judgement and lead to choices that cause pain and suffering—not only for ourselves but for others. In Bharthari's case, his deep attachment to Pingala led him to overlook her flaws and fall victim to betrayal.

The second lesson is the impermanence of worldly attachments. Just as the fruit passed from one person to another, so too do worldly pleasures. Wealth, love, power—these things are never truly ours to keep. They can easily be taken away, or in some cases, betray us, leaving us empty and disillusioned. Bharthari's story reminds us that the only lasting peace comes from within, through self-knowledge and detachment from the illusions of the material world.

The final lesson is the value of renunciation. Bharthari's decision to leave his kingdom and embrace the life of an ascetic was not an act of defeat, but one of profound realisation. He understood that true happiness does not come from external possessions or relationships, but from the inner journey of understanding oneself and one's true nature.

The story of Bharthari and Pingala serves as a powerful reminder of the perils of unchecked desire and the ultimate freedom that comes from renouncing the fleeting pleasures of the world. Bharthari's journey—from a king bound by lust and love to a wise sage who saw through the illusions of life—teaches us that wisdom, self-control, and detachment are the keys to true liberation.

By turning away from lust and the material world, Bharthari was able to find a deeper sense of peace and fulfilment. His writings, particularly the "Niti Satakam," continue to inspire those seeking to overcome the distractions of desire and walk the path of spiritual wisdom. In the end, Bharthari's story shows us that while the fruit of lust may be tempting, it ultimately leads to suffering—only wisdom and renunciation can bring lasting joy.

THE STORY OF THE BLINDFOLDED SEEKERS (KENO- UPANISHAD)

In the sacred land where rivers of wisdom flowed through the hearts of seekers, a group of sages gathered to ponder the greatest question of all: "What is the source of life? What gives power to our eyes, our thoughts, and our breath?"

These seekers were no ordinary students. They were scholars, philosophers, and wise men who had spent their entire lives studying the scriptures, meditating, and seeking the truth. Yet, despite all their efforts, they were unable to grasp the essence of what they sought. They had mastered the world of the senses—the ability to see, hear, touch, and think—but they still felt an emptiness, a gap in their understanding.

One day, they decided to conduct an unusual experiment. They would each blindfold themselves, depriving themselves of sight and sound, hoping to find a deeper reality beyond their senses. "Perhaps," they thought, "if we let go of what we see and hear, we will discover what lies beyond."

The Blindfolded Test

With their eyes covered, the seekers sat in silence. Their ears strained for sound, but all they heard was the rustle of the wind. Their hands reached out into the darkness, but they grasped nothing. Time seemed to stretch on endlessly, and the more they waited, the more they felt disconnected from the world around them.

At first, there was frustration. "How can we understand anything without our senses?" one of the seekers wondered aloud. "We see the world with our eyes, we hear the teachings with our ears. Without them, how can we know anything?"

But the leader of the group, an old sage with deep wisdom, replied softly, "It is not the eyes that truly see, nor the ears that truly hear. There is something deeper, something unseen, which allows the eyes to see and the ears to hear. That is what we must seek."

The Appearance of Brahman

As the blindfolded seekers sat in the stillness, something remarkable began to happen. Though their eyes were covered, they started to perceive a presence, a subtle force, not through their senses, but through an inner awareness. It was as if a light, brighter than anything they had ever seen with their eyes, began to glow within them.

This presence was Brahman, the **ultimate reality,** the invisible force that powers all perception and thought. It was not something that could be seen or heard, but it was the very foundation of all seeing and hearing.

The seekers, in their silence and blindness, realised a profound truth: Brahman was "that which cannot be seen by the eye, but by which the eye sees; that which cannot be heard by the ear, but by which the ear hears." This was the secret revealed by the Kena Upanishad. Brahman was beyond all forms, beyond all senses, yet it was the source of everything.

The Divine Revelation

Suddenly, everything became clear. The seekers understood that all their senses and intellect, no matter how sharp or refined, could never truly grasp the nature of Brahman. Brahman was the unseen force behind all perception. The eye sees only because Brahman gives it the power to see; the mind thinks only because Brahman allows it to think. Brahman was not an object to be known, but the very essence of knowing itself.

The blindfolded seekers were filled with awe. They realised they had spent their lives searching for Brahman through the senses and intellect, but Brahman was beyond all that. It was everywhere, yet nowhere to be found. It was not something they could capture, measure, or even fully understand. It could only be experienced, like the stillness in the silence, like the unseen wind that moves the leaves.

The Lesson of Humility:

The seekers, who had once been proud of their knowledge, now felt a deep sense of humility. They had thought that through their learning and meditation, they could come to possess the truth. But now they understood that Brahman, the ultimate reality, was beyond possession. It could not be owned, controlled, or fully explained.

They realised that the mind, brilliant as it may be, was limited. The senses, powerful as they are, can only show the surface of things. True wisdom lies not in the mastery of the senses, but in the surrender to the mystery of Brahman. To know Brahman is not to explain it, but to experience it in silence, humility, and surrender.

Reflection and Key Takeaways

The story of the blindfolded seekers from the Kena Upanishad teaches a profound lesson about the nature of reality and the limits of human knowledge. Brahman, the ultimate truth, cannot be grasped by the senses or the intellect. The eye can only see physical forms, the ear can only hear sounds, and the mind can only think thoughts, but Brahman is beyond all of these.

The Upanishads teach us that while we rely on our senses and intellect to navigate the world, they are not the final authority on truth. There is a deeper reality, a divine presence, which is the source of all perception and thought. Brahman is that invisible force which powers our consciousness, but it cannot be seen, touched, or fully understood by the mind.

This chapter invites readers to reflect on their own search for truth. Are we blindfolded by our attachment to the senses and intellect, trying to grasp something that is beyond their reach? The path to true wisdom requires not just learning, but also humility—the recognition that some truths cannot be explained, only experienced.

Allow me to shift the narrative from the Kena Upanishad to a hypothetical tale. The intention is not to distort the original story but to clarify the message, ensuring that the book's purpose remains intact.

The Blindfolded Seekers (Extension 2)

In a bustling village nestled in the heart of ancient India, there lived five curious friends: Aditi, Bhanu, Chandra, Devi, and Eshan. They were known throughout the land for their insatiable thirst for knowledge and their constant debates about the nature of reality.

One day, a wise sage named Guru Vidya visited their village. The friends, excited by the prospect of gaining new wisdom, approached the guru with a burning question:

"O wise one," Aditi began, "we have spent years discussing and arguing about the true nature of Brahman, the ultimate reality. Yet, we seem no closer to understanding it. Can you enlighten us?"

Guru Vidya smiled mysteriously and replied, "My dear seekers, your question is profound. But instead of giving you an answer, I shall give you an experience. Meet me at the village square at dawn tomorrow, and bring clean clothes to cover your eyes."

The friends, intrigued and slightly puzzled, agreed.

The next morning, they gathered in the misty village square. Guru Vidya approached them, holding a large, peculiar object covered with a silk cloth.

"Today," the guru announced, "you will attempt to understand the nature of this object. But there's a catch – you must do so while blindfolded, using only your sense of touch."

The friends excitedly tied the clothes around their eyes and gathered around the mysterious object.

Guru Vidya guided Aditi's hand to touch one part of the object. "It's long and cylindrical," Aditi exclaimed, "like a sturdy pillar!"

Next, Bhanu touched another part. "No, no," he disagreed, "it's flat and wide, like a giant leaf!"

Chandra felt yet another section. "You're both wrong," she insisted, "it's thin and rope-like!"

Devi's turn came, and she touched a different area. "It's none of those things," she argued, "it feels rough and hard, like tree bark!"

Finally, Eshan explored the object. "I disagree with all of you," he declared confidently, "it's clearly flexible and fan-like!"

As the friends began to argue amongst themselves, each convinced of their own perception, Guru Vidya raised a hand for silence.

"Remove your blindfolds," the sage instructed gently.

As the clothes fell away, the friends gasped in astonishment. Before them stood a majestic elephant, patiently enduring their explorations.

"Aditi," Guru Vidya explained, "you touched the elephant's leg. Bhanu, you felt its ear. Chandra, you held its tail. Devi, you explored its trunk, and Eshan, you touched its ear from a different angle."

The friends stood in shocked silence, realising how limited their individual perceptions had been.

"Just as each of you experienced only a small part of the elephant," Guru Vidya continued, "so too do we perceive only fragments of the ultimate reality, Brahman. Our senses and intellect, like your blindfolded explorations, can grasp only parts of the whole."

The sage's eyes twinkled with wisdom as he concluded, "The Kena Upanishad teaches us that Brahman is beyond the reach of our senses and ordinary consciousness. It is that by which our eyes see, our ears hear, and our minds think, yet it cannot be fully comprehended by these faculties alone."

The friends looked at each other, humbled by the profound lesson.

"Then how can we ever hope to understand Brahman?" Aditi asked softly.

Guru Vidya smiled. "By recognizing the limitations of our perceptions and knowledge, we take the first step towards true wisdom. The path to understanding Brahman lies not in grasping it with our minds, but in opening ourselves to experience it directly, beyond the blindfolds of our limited senses and thoughts."

As the sun rose higher in the sky, casting a golden light over the village square, the five friends bowed to Guru Vidya with newfound respect and humility. They realised that their journey of understanding had only just begun, and that the greatest wisdom lay in recognizing how much they had yet to learn.

From that day forward, Aditi, Bhanu, Chandra, Devi, and Eshan approached their search for knowledge with open minds and hearts, always remembering the lesson of the blindfolded seekers and the elephant.

THE SEEKER'S FLAME: WISDOM FROM THE MUNDAKA UPANISHAD

In the depths of ignorance, a single question can ignite the flame of wisdom. Are you ready to light the lamp of knowledge within?

In the ashram of the great sage Angiras, seekers of truth gathered from far and wide. Among them was Shaunaka, a wealthy householder known for his deep thirst for wisdom. As the golden rays of dawn kissed the earth, Shaunaka approached Angiras with folded hands and a humble heart.

"Revered teacher," Shaunaka began, his voice quivering with anticipation, "I have studied the Vedas, performed countless rituals, and lived a life of dharma. Yet, a void persists in my heart. Tell me, what is that by knowing which all else is known?"

Angiras, his eyes twinkling with the light of realisation, smiled gently. "Ah, Shaunaka, you have asked the most profound question. Listen carefully, for the answer lies beyond the realm of ordinary knowledge."

The sage continued, his words resonating with ancient wisdom:

द्वे विद्ये वेदितव्ये इति ह स्म यद्ब्रह्मविदो वदन्ति परा चैवापरा च ।

(dve vidye veditavye iti ha sma yadbrahmavido vadanti parā caivāparā ca)

"Two kinds of knowledge must be known, as the knowers of Brahman declare - the higher and the lower." (Mundaka Upanishad)

"The lower knowledge, Shaunaka, consists of the Rig Veda, Yajur Veda, Sama Veda, Atharva Veda, and all the sciences. It is like a raft that can take you across the river of worldly existence, but it cannot lead you to the ocean of supreme truth."

Shaunaka listened intently, realising that his vast learning was but a stepping stone to something far greater.

Angiras's voice deepened as he revealed the higher knowledge:

यत्तददद्रेश्यमग्राह्यमगोत्रमवर्णमचक्षुश्रोत्रं तदपाणिपादम् ।

नित्यं विभुं सर्वगतं सुसूक्ष्मं तदव्ययं यद्भूतयोनिं परिपश्यन्ति धीराः ॥

(yattadadreśyamagrāhyamagotramavarṇamaca
kṣuḥśrotraṃ tadapāṇipādam

nityaṃ vibhuṃ sarvagataṃ susūkṣmaṃ
tadavyayaṃ yadbhūtayoniṃ paripaśyanti
dhīrāḥ)

"That which is invisible, ungraspable, without family or caste, without eyes or ears, hands or feet, eternal, all-pervading, omnipresent, and extremely subtle - that is the Immutable, which the wise perceive as the source of all creation." (Mundaka Upanishad

As these words washed over Shaunaka, he felt a stirring in his soul, as if a long-dormant flame had been kindled.

Angiras, seeing the light of understanding dawn in Shaunaka's eyes, shared a powerful metaphor:

यथोर्णनाभिःसृजते गृह्णते च यथा पृथिव्यामोषधयः सम्भवन्ति।

यथा सतःपुरुषात्केशलोमानितथाऽक्षरात्सम्भवतीह
विश्वम् ॥

(yathorṇanābhiḥ sṛjate gṛhṇate ca yathā
pṛthivyāmoṣadhayaḥ sambhavanti

yathā sataḥ puruṣātkeśalomāni
tathā'kṣarātsambhavatīha viśvam)

"As a spider spins and withdraws its web, as herbs grow from the earth, as hair grows from the head and body of a living person, so does the universe emerge from the Immutable." (Mundaka Upanishad)

Shaunaka's mind reeled with the profound implications of this teaching. He realised that the truth he sought was not separate from himself, but the very essence of his being.

Angiras, seeing the transformation in his disciple, concluded with words that would echo through eternity:

सत्येन लभ्यस्तपसा ह्येष आत्मा सम्यग्ज्ञानेन
ब्रह्मचर्येण नित्यम् ।

(satyena labhyastapasā hyeṣa ātmā
samyagjñānena brahmacaryeṇa nityam)

"This Atman is to be realised by the constant practice of truthfulness, austerity, correct knowledge, and continence." (Mundaka Upanishad)

As the sun reached its zenith, Shaunaka bowed deeply to his teacher, his heart aflame with the light of wisdom. He understood that his journey had only just begun, but now he held the map to the ultimate treasure - the knowledge of the Self.

Reflection

The Mundaka Upanishad, through the dialogue between Angiras and Shaunaka, illuminates the path from ignorance to enlightenment. It teaches us that true wisdom lies beyond mere intellectual knowledge or ritualistic practices. The higher knowledge, the understanding of Brahman or the ultimate reality, is what liberates us from the cycle of birth and death.

This ancient text encourages us to look beyond the apparent, to seek the invisible thread that connects all existence. It reminds us that the greatest truths are often the simplest, hidden in plain sight within our own being.

The metaphor of the spider's web beautifully illustrates the concept of creation and dissolution. Just as a spider effortlessly creates its web from its own substance and then reabsorbs it, the entire universe emerges from and dissolves back into the Immutable Brahman. This imagery invites us to contemplate our own nature and our relationship with the cosmos.

Moreover, the Upanishad emphasises that this supreme knowledge is not merely theoretical but must be lived. The path to realisation involves truthfulness, austerity, correct knowledge, and self-control. It's a call to align our thoughts, words, and actions with the highest truth.

In our modern world, filled with distractions and superficial knowledge, the wisdom of the Mundaka Upanishad serves as a beacon. It reminds us to turn our gaze inward, to seek the eternal amidst the transient, and to recognize the divine spark within ourselves and all beings.

As we reflect on these teachings, let us ask ourselves: What is the nature of true knowledge? How can we move beyond the limitations of our senses and mind to perceive the underlying reality? How might our lives transform if we lived with the constant awareness of our divine essence?

May the flame of wisdom kindled by these ancient words guide us on our journey from the unreal to the real, from darkness to light, from death to immortality.

THE DREAMER AND THE DREAMED" (BASED ON MANDUKYA UPANISHAD)

The Mandukya Upanishad is one of the shortest Upanishads, consisting of just 12 verses. Despite its brevity, it is considered one of the most profound texts in Hindu philosophy. It focuses on the sacred syllable OM and its relationship to the nature of consciousness and reality.

The text begins by stating that OM represents all of existence - past, present, and future - and even that which is beyond time. It then breaks down OM into four parts, each corresponding to a state of consciousness:

1. Vaishvanara - The Waking State: This is our normal, everyday consciousness. We experience the world through our senses and interact with objects around us. In this state, we identify ourselves as separate individuals.

2. Taijasa - The Dreaming State: When we sleep and dream, we experience a world created by our mind. Our consciousness turns inward, creating vivid experiences that feel real while we're dreaming.

3. Prajna - The Deep Sleep State: In deep, dreamless sleep, we experience no desires and no dream images. There's a state of undifferentiated consciousness, where the sense of individual self temporarily dissolves.
4. Turiya - The Fourth State: This is the state beyond the other three. It's not a state we "enter" but rather the underlying reality that is always present. It's pure consciousness, beyond words and concepts.

The Mandukya Upanishad teaches that these four states are not separate realities, but different expressions of the same consciousness. The true Self (Atman) is the witness of all these states, unchanged by them.

In the waking state, we think we are separate individuals interacting with the real world. In the dream state, we create entire worlds that feel just as real. In deep sleep, we lose all sense of individuality. But in all these states, there is something that knows these experiences - pure awareness itself.

The profound teaching of the Upanishad is that this pure awareness, Turiya, is our true nature. It's not something to be achieved but to be recognized. We are not just the dreamer creating dream worlds; we are also not limited to being the individual experiencing the waking world. We are the unchanging consciousness that knows all these states.

This realisation leads to the understanding of non-duality (Advaita). The dreamer and the dreamed are one. The individual self and the universal Self are one. All of existence is a manifestation of the same consciousness.

The practical implication of this teaching is profound. By recognizing our true nature as pure consciousness, we can free ourselves from the limitations and sufferings of identifying solely with the body and mind. We can live with a sense of peace and unity, seeing the divine in everything.

The Mandukya Upanishad invites us to look beyond our usual perception of reality. It challenges us to question our assumptions about who we are and what the world is. By contemplating these teachings and exploring our own consciousness, we can discover the eternal truth that has been with us all along - that we are not separate from the universe, but are the very awareness in which all existence appears.

Let us try to understand this with a great story

The Profound Tale of Raja Janak's Spiritual Journey

In the ancient land of Videha, located in the Mithila region of India, there ruled a king named Janak. Known for his wisdom and spiritual inclination, Raja Janak was not merely a ruler of lands but a seeker of the ultimate truth. His story is a testament to the harmonious blend of royal duties and spiritual aspirations, a narrative that delves deep into the nature of reality, consciousness, and the self.

The Curious King Janak

Janak was no ordinary monarch. While he governed his kingdom with justice and compassion, his heart yearned for something beyond the material realm. He was intensely interested in spiritual discourse and considered himself free from worldly illusions. This unique disposition led him to contemplate renouncing his kingdom to live as an ascetic, dedicating his life entirely to spiritual pursuits.

However, fate had different plans for Janak. His spiritual guru, the great sage Yajnavalkya, advised him against abandoning his royal duties. Yajnavalkya, recognizing the unique position

Janak held, suggested that he continue as a king for the welfare of his state and people. The sage explained that Janak's time was not yet ripe to leave his kingdom, as his self-knowledge was incomplete. He needed to learn the profound lessons of Brahman from the sage Ashtavakra before taking the final step towards complete renunciation.

The Path of a Spiritual King

Heeding his guru's advice, Janak agreed to continue his role as a king while pursuing his spiritual journey. This decision set the stage for a remarkable experiment in governance - a king who ruled with detachment, seeing his royal duties as a form of spiritual practice.

Janak's court became a hub of spiritual and philosophical discourse. He regularly invited erudite scholars to debate on the nature of ultimate truth. These gatherings were not mere intellectual exercises but intense sessions where the deepest questions of existence were probed. It was through these associations with great intellectuals and his dedicated practice based on religious teachings that Janak had mastered all the scriptures.

Yet, a question lingered in his mind - was this knowledge enough?

In his quest for deeper understanding, Raja Janak began attending the discourses of the sage Ashtavakra. It was during one such session that an event occurred which would become legendary in spiritual circles.

As Janak sat absorbed in Ashtavakra's words, one of his courtiers came running, panic evident in his voice. "Maharaj! Your palace is burning!" he exclaimed. The entire assembly was thrown into commotion, but Janak remained unmoved. He continued listening to Ashtavakra, showing no reaction to the news of his burning palace.

Astonished by this display of detachment, Ashtavakra paused his discourse. He used this moment to illustrate to everyone present the science of non-attachment that Janak had mastered. Here was a king who, even when faced with the loss of his grand palace, remained focused on spiritual truth.

The Dream and the Question

Janak's spiritual journey took an even more profound turn one night when he had a vivid dream. In this dream, he saw himself dethroned, exiled, and wandering in difficult terrain through a jungle. Hungry, exhausted, and thirsty, he reached a bordering country.

There, he saw some poor people being fed rice and lentils by a rich man. Desperate for food, Janak joined the queue. By the time his turn came, only a small amount of soup remained at the bottom of the vessel. As the man was about to offer this last bit of soup to Janak, a kite came tumbling down, hitting the bowl and throwing it into the mud.

"Save me! Save me!" Janak screamed in his dream, waking up his queen. Concerned, she asked him what was wrong. Janak, still caught between the dream world and waking reality, posed a question that would become central to his spiritual inquiry: "Was that a dream, or is this a dream?"

This experience led Janak to contemplate deeply on the nature of reality. He wondered, "Is this the truth? Or is that the truth?" The line between what he perceived as real in his waking state and what he experienced in his dream became blurred, leading him to question the very nature of existence.

The Philosophical Implications

Janak's question - "Was that a dream, or is this a dream?" - is not merely a result of confusion but a profound philosophical inquiry. It touches upon the core of Advaita Vedanta philosophy, which posits that the waking world is as illusory as the dream world from the perspective of ultimate reality or Brahman.

This experience led Janak to explore the concept of Turiya, the fourth state of consciousness beyond waking, dreaming, and deep sleep. As explained in the Mandukya Upanishad, Turiya is a state that is:

"Not inwardly cognitive, nor outwardly cognitive, not both-wise cognitive, not a cognition-mass, not cognitive, not non-cognitive, unseen, with which there can be no dealing, ungraspable, having no distinctive mark, non-thinkable, that cannot be designated, the essence of the assurance of which is the state of being one with the Self, the cessation of development, tranquil, benign, without a second."

Janak's journey from a curious king to a realised sage illustrates the path to this ultimate state of consciousness. His story demonstrates that true detachment is not about physically renouncing the world, but about maintaining equanimity in all situations, whether perceived as favourable or unfavourable.

Reflection:

Raja Janak's life and spiritual journey serve as a profound example of how one can pursue the highest truth while fulfilling worldly responsibilities. His story challenges the notion that spiritual enlightenment is the exclusive domain of renunciates and ascetics.

By maintaining his role as a king while pursuing spiritual knowledge, Janak demonstrated that it is possible to be in the world but not of it. His ability to remain unperturbed in the face of both potential calamity (the burning palace) and illusory suffering (the dream) showcases the state of a true Karma Yogi - one who performs actions without attachment to their fruits.

Janak's philosophical inquiries and experiences continue to inspire seekers of truth. His question about the nature of reality and the state of consciousness he achieved serve as guideposts for those navigating the complex terrain of spiritual awakening.

In essence, the story of Raja Janak is not just a tale from ancient India, but a timeless narrative that speaks to the human quest for understanding the nature of existence, consciousness, and the self. It reminds us that true wisdom lies not in escaping our worldly duties, but in performing them with detachment and awareness, always keeping our gaze fixed on the ultimate truth.

Let me take this liberty to highlight certain stories from the Puranas, Ramayan , and Mahabharta that complement the teachings of the Upanishads. These stories add more meaning and illustrate important lessons that resonate with the deep insights found in the Upanishads. By exploring these narratives, I aim to show how the wisdom of the scriptures enhances our understanding of spiritual truths. This connection between the Various literatures invites readers to explore the timeless lessons that continue to inspire and guide us today.

The Descent of the Ganga (Ganga Avataran)

In a land parched by time, where ancient kings ruled with might and wisdom, one man's unyielding determination changed the course of history. The earth cried for relief, and the heavens held the answer—but only a soul pure in its purpose, driven by boundless perseverance and humility, could bring the celestial river down from the heavens. This is the epic tale of King Bhagiratha, whose devotion and sacrifices brought the sacred Ganga from the skies to the earth, giving life not only to his ancestors but to all of humanity.

The story of Ganga's descent begins in the distant past, when a great calamity befell the kingdom of King Sagara, an illustrious ruler of the Ikshvaku dynasty. King Sagara, desiring to establish his power and fame, performed the Ashwamedha Yajna, the horse sacrifice ritual. The sacrificial horse, an emblem of his sovereignty, was set free to roam, but was stolen by none other than the king of the heavens, Indra.

As the king's 60,000 sons searched for the horse, they finally found it tied near the hermitage of Sage Kapila. Overcome by anger, they accused the sage of theft. Kapila, absorbed in meditation, opened his eyes, and with the intensity of his inner power, reduced all 60,000 sons to ashes. Their souls, trapped in limbo, could not ascend to the heavens. The only way to release them from their suffering was through the purifying waters of the Ganga, the river of the gods.

King Bhagiratha's Vow

Generations passed, but the souls of the 60,000 sons remained in torment. Then came Bhagiratha, a descendant of King Sagara, a noble and compassionate king who vowed to release his ancestors from this fate. Bhagiratha knew that only the sacred waters of Ganga, descending from the heavens, could purify the ashes of his ancestors and free them from the curse.

Determined to fulfil this task, Bhagiratha renounced his kingdom and all worldly pleasures, embarking on an arduous penance. He stood motionless in the midst of scorching summers and freezing winters, offering prayers to the creator, Brahma, seeking his blessing to bring the Ganga down from the heavens. For years, Bhagiratha's Tapasya (austerities) continued, and eventually, Brahma appeared before him.

Moved by Bhagiratha's unwavering devotion, Brahma granted his wish but warned him of a great challenge. If the Ganga descended directly onto the earth, her force would be so immense that she would shatter the planet. Only Lord Shiva could bear the full force of the Ganga's descent.

The Plea to Lord Shiva

With newfound hope, Bhagiratha redirected his penance toward Lord Shiva. Once again, years passed as Bhagiratha remained steadfast in his prayers, calling upon the supreme deity. Finally, Lord Shiva appeared, his presence as calming as the moonlight and as powerful as a storm. With humility, Bhagiratha pleaded with Shiva to catch Ganga in his matted hair, preventing her from devastating the earth.

Moved by Bhagiratha's devotion and his noble purpose, Lord Shiva agreed. As the heavens opened and Ganga began her descent, Lord Shiva extended his locks, catching the mighty river. Ganga's turbulent waters swirled and twisted in Shiva's hair, becoming calm and manageable. Only after Shiva released her gently did Ganga begin to flow toward the earth.

The River's Journey to Earth

Ganga flowed gracefully from the heavens, her divine waters bringing life wherever they touched. But Bhagiratha's journey was not yet complete. As the river made her way to the ashes of the 60,000 ancestors, she encountered many obstacles. Along her path, Ganga flooded fields, disrupted sages, and altered the landscape.

One such obstacle was Sage Jahnu, whose hermitage lay in the river's path. Angered by Ganga's unruly flood, Jahnu drank the entire river. Bhagiratha, once again undeterred, prayed to the sage for mercy. Jahnu, impressed by Bhagiratha's persistence and respectful plea, released the river from his ear, allowing her to continue. From that day, Ganga was also known as Jahnavi, the daughter of Sage Jahnu.

Finally, after years of penance and countless trials, Bhagiratha led Ganga to the spot where the ashes of his ancestors lay. The river, with her divine waters, washed over the ashes, purifying them and releasing the souls of the 60,000 sons of King Sagara from their curse. Their souls ascended to the heavens, free at last.

Reflection on the Story: The Power of Perseverance and Sacrifice

The story of King Bhagiratha and the descent of the Ganga is one of the most profound in Indian spiritual literature. It symbolises the power of perseverance, sacrifice, and humility in the face of seemingly insurmountable challenges. Bhagiratha's determination to liberate his ancestors is a testament to selfless devotion. His mission was not for personal gain, but for the salvation of others—a theme that resonates deeply with the principles of dharma (righteousness) and karma (the law of action).

The story teaches us that a noble goal, pursued with sincerity and humility, can have far-reaching benefits beyond the individual. Bhagiratha's efforts brought the sacred Ganga not only for the salvation of his ancestors but also for all of humanity. To this day, the Ganga is revered as a life-giving force, a purifier of sins, and a symbol of divine grace.

The significance of Ganga's descent is highlighted in various texts, including the **Valmiki Ramayana,** where it is written:

Ganga devi, pure and sacred, descended from the heavens to purify the sins of the world and cleanse the souls of Bhagiratha's ancestors.

Another verse from the **Shiva Purana** emphasises the greatness of Bhagiratha's perseverance:

By the power of his unwavering penance and the grace of Lord Shiva, Bhagiratha brought the river of the gods to earth, purifying both heaven and earth."

Conclusion: Lessons for Life

The story of Bhagiratha and the descent of Ganga offers a timeless lesson in the importance of dedication and perseverance. In a world where we often face challenges that seem beyond our control, Bhagiratha's journey reminds us that persistence, combined with humility and a sense of higher purpose, can overcome even the greatest obstacles.

Just as Bhagiratha's efforts brought divine blessings not just to his ancestors but to all of humanity, our actions—if rooted in righteousness—can create ripples that positively impact others. His story is a reminder that every noble endeavour requires patience and sacrifice, but in the end, the rewards can benefit generations to come.

The descent of Ganga is not merely a mythological tale; it is a spiritual allegory for how the grace of the divine can flow into our lives when we are willing to endure, to sacrifice, and to act with purity of heart. Ganga continues to be a symbol of divine grace and the power of selfless action, a legacy that endures as long as her waters flow across the land.

THE STORY OF THE SAMUDRA MANTHAN

The story of the Samudra Manthan, the churning of the ocean, is one of the most captivating tales from the Vishnu Purana. It offers deep insights into human nature, cosmic balance, and the eternal interplay between good and evil. It's more than just an ancient myth; it reflects our daily struggles, victories, and challenges.

The Setting of the Cosmic Churn:

Once, a conflict broke out between the Devas (gods) and Asuras (demons) over who would rule the heavens. The Devas, gradually losing strength, realised they needed divine help to restore balance. They turned to Lord Vishnu, the Preserver of the Universe, for guidance. Vishnu, in his wisdom, suggested a solution: "Churn the ocean of milk, the Ksheera Sagara, to extract the nectar of immortality, Amrita." This nectar would grant them the power they needed to defeat the Asuras.

The catch? The gods couldn't do it alone. They needed the cooperation of the Asuras, their sworn enemies.

Though uneasy, the Devas knew they had to team up with their foes. So, they approached the Asuras with a promise to share the nectar. The Asuras, hungry for immortality, agreed, and the great churning of the ocean—Samudra Manthan—was set in motion.

Preparation for the Great Churning:

The cosmic task required immense resources. They chose Mount Mandara as the churning rod, but it was so colossal that neither the gods nor the demons could move it. Seeing their struggle, Lord Vishnu summoned Garuda, his mighty eagle, who lifted the mountain and placed it in the ocean.

For the churning rope, they chose the powerful serpent Vasuki. The Asuras, in their pride, insisted on holding Vasuki's head, while the Devas wisely took the tail. As the churning began, the pressure of the enormous mountain sinking into the ocean disrupted the process. But Vishnu, once again, intervened by taking the form of Kurma, the giant tortoise, and supported the mountain on his back, balancing the cosmos.

In this divine act, the forces of nature aligned with the spiritual world, reminding us of the delicate balance between the material and the divine.

"The serpent king (Vasuki) became the churning rope, and Mandara, the churning rod, while the Devas and the foremost of the Daityas churned the ocean tirelessly."

Just like the unyielding effort of the gods and demons in this verse, the back-and-forth motion of the churning represents the constant tug-of-war in our own lives—between ambition and patience, joy and sorrow, success and failure.

The Treasures and the Poison:

As the churning continued, wonders began to emerge from the ocean, symbolising life's unexpected rewards. First, Kamadhenu, the wish-fulfilling cow, appeared. Then came Airavata, the divine white elephant, followed by Kalpavriksha, the tree that grants every desire, and even Goddess Lakshmi, the goddess of wealth and fortune, who chose Vishnu as her consort.

But with the good comes the bad. Among the treasures rose the deadliest substance known to the universe: Halahala, a venom so toxic that it threatened to destroy all creation. This poison is a powerful metaphor for the inevitable obstacles we face when striving toward our goals. Just as in life, no great reward comes without significant challenges.

The gods and demons were powerless against this deadly poison. In desperation, they turned to Lord Shiva, the ultimate destroyer and protector of the cosmos. Without hesitation, Shiva took the poison in his hands and swallowed it to save the universe. But as the poison reached his throat, his wife, Goddess Parvati, stopped it from descending further, turning his throat blue. From then on, Shiva came to be known as Neelkanth, the blue-throated one.

By his grace, Shiva, with his resplendent neck, effortlessly drank the Halahala poison, storing it in his throat, thus saving the world.

This act of selflessness teaches a crucial lesson: even in the pursuit of success, we must be prepared to face toxicity—whether it be criticism, setbacks, or personal sacrifice. Shiva's grace in containing the poison reminds us of the power of detachment and sacrifice.

The Nectar of Immortality:

Finally, after much struggle and perseverance, the gods and demons were rewarded. Dhanvantari, the divine physician, emerged from the depths of the ocean holding the Amrita, the nectar of immortality. Eager to claim it, the Asuras seized the pot. But Vishnu, ever wise, transformed into the mesmerising form of Mohini, an enchantress so beautiful that the Asuras were bewitched by her charm.

Under the guise of fairness, Mohini offered to distribute the nectar to both parties. However, she only gave it to the Devas, ensuring that they alone would drink the Amrita and gain immortality. The Asuras, distracted by her beauty, did not realise the deception until it was too late.

One Asura, Rahu, disguised himself as a Deva and managed to drink some nectar. But before he could swallow it fully, the Sun and Moon exposed his deception. Vishnu, in the form of Mohini, beheaded Rahu. However, because he had consumed some of the nectar, his head became immortal, and Rahu continued to chase the Sun and Moon,

Reflections on Samudra Manthan:

The story of the churning of the ocean is a profound metaphor for the human experience. It teaches that perseverance is key to achieving any goal. The gods and demons had to churn tirelessly, facing obstacles and rewards alike, to achieve their ultimate prize.

In the same way, we must continue to "churn" through life's difficulties. The poison that emerged represents the inevitable hardships we face. Just as Lord Shiva's act of swallowing the poison saved the world, we too must be willing to take on challenges and sacrifices for the greater good, keeping our focus on the larger goal.

Moreover, the cooperation between the gods and demons highlights the need for balance. The dualities of life—light and dark, good and evil— are not separate; they coexist and must often work together for something meaningful to emerge. Both sides of life are necessary, and even when faced with opposition, it is through their cooperation that the nectar of immortality is found.

Lastly, faith in divine intervention plays a central role. Whether it is Lord Vishnu supporting the mountain as Kurma or transforming into Mohini to deceive the Asuras, the divine steps in to ensure the balance of the cosmos. This suggests that in times of great struggle, faith and surrender to a higher power can bring resolution beyond our own abilities.

In conclusion, the story of the Samudra Manthan serves as a powerful allegory for life. It reflects the perseverance required to succeed, the balance between opposing forces, and the challenges we must overcome. In our journey, we will encounter treasures and poisons alike, but through patience, cooperation, and faith, we can extract the nectar of life's ultimate rewards.

The Story of Dhruva – Vishnu Purana

Have you ever felt a burning desire so strong that it consumed your every thought, your every breath? A desire so powerful that it could move mountains, part seas, and even touch the very fabric of the universe? This is the extraordinary tale of Balak Dhruv, a young boy whose indomitable spirit and unwavering faith shook the cosmos and etched his name in the annals of time.

The Seeds of Destiny

In the golden age of ancient India, there ruled a mighty king named Uttanpada. His kingdom was vast and prosperous, stretching from the snow-capped peaks of the Himalayas to the sun-kissed shores of the southern seas. But within the opulent walls of his grand palace, a story of love, jealousy, and destiny was about to unfold.

King Uttanpada had two queens: Suniti and Suruchi. Suruchi, with her bewitching beauty and clever words, had captured the king's heart, becoming his favorite. Her melodious laughter echoed through the palace halls, her every wish instantly granted. In stark contrast, Suniti, though equally beautiful and far more virtuous, found herself relegated to the shadows, her gentle voice often drowned out by the court's clamor.

Each queen bore the king a son. Suruchi's son, Uttama, grew up basking in the warmth of royal privilege. His every whim was indulged, his every tantrum soothed with lavish gifts. On the other hand, Suniti's son, Dhruv, though loved deeply by his mother, felt the chill of neglect from his father and the rest of the court.

The Spark of Determination

As the seasons changed and years passed, young Dhruv's heart grew heavy with questions. Why did his father's eyes light up at the sight of Uttama but barely flicker when he entered the room? Why did the courtiers bow deeply to his half-brother while merely nodding in his direction? The innocent child's mind couldn't comprehend the complex web of adult emotions and politics that surrounded him.

One fateful day, when Dhruv was merely five years old, he wandered into the royal court. His eyes widened with wonder at the sight of his father, King Uttanpada, sitting regally on his golden throne. Beside him sat Queen Suruchi, resplendent in her jewels, while Prince Uttama nestled comfortably on the king's lap.

A sudden longing gripped Dhruv's heart. How he wished to feel his father's loving embrace, to sit upon that strong lap and hear words of affection whispered in his ear! With the innocent courage that only a child possesses, he stepped forward, his little hands reaching out towards his father.

But before he could take another step, Queen Suruchi's sharp voice cut through the air like a whip. "Stop right there, little prince," she said, her words dripping with false sweetness. "That exalted seat is not for you. Only a child born of my womb deserves to sit on the king's lap and inherit his throne."

The court fell silent, the tension palpable. King Uttanpada, weak-willed and besotted, remained quiet, neither defending his son nor rebuking his wife. Dhruv stood frozen, his small frame trembling, his eyes brimming with unshed tears.

Suruchi, emboldened by the king's silence, continued, "If you truly desire such an honor, you should pray to be reborn as my son in your next life. Perhaps then, you'll be worthy of the king's affection."

The Seed of Devotion Sprouts

With those cruel words ringing in his ears, Dhruv ran from the court, his little feet carrying him through the winding palace corridors until he reached his mother's chambers. He flung himself into Suniti's arms, his body wracked with sobs as he recounted the humiliation he had endured.

Suniti's heart broke for her son, but she knew that bitterness and revenge would only poison his pure soul. With tears glistening in her eyes, she gently lifted Dhruv's chin, meeting his gaze with a look of unwavering love and wisdom.

"My precious child," she said, her voice soft yet strong, "the path to greatness is not through hatred or jealousy. If you truly wish to reach the highest place, one that no one can take away from you, seek the blessings of Lord Vishnu. His love knows no boundaries of birth or status. Devote yourself to Him, and you will find a place far beyond any earthly throne."

These words, spoken with a mother's love and a devotee's faith, planted a seed in young Dhruv's heart. As he lay in bed that night, sleep eluding him, he made a decision that would alter the course of his life and inspire generations to come.

The Journey Begins

Under the cover of darkness, with nothing but the clothes on his back and his mother's words echoing in his mind, five-year-old Dhruv slipped out of the palace. The night was moonless, the path ahead obscured by shadows, but the fire of determination burning in his heart lit the way.

As he stepped into the forest that bordered the kingdom, the sounds of civilization faded, replaced by the mysterious symphony of the wild. Owls hooted ominously, unseen creatures rustled in the underbrush, and the wind whispered secrets through the leaves. Any other child would have been paralyzed with fear, but Dhruv pressed on, his small feet leaving imprints on the forest floor.

Days blended into nights as Dhruv ventured deeper into the wilderness. He forded streams, his tiny body shivering in the cold water. He climbed hills, his muscles aching but his spirit unyielding. When hunger gnawed at his stomach, he ate fallen berries and leaves. When thirst parched his throat, he cupped his hands to drink from clear brooks.

All the while, one name remained on his lips, a constant mantra that sustained him through every hardship: "Vishnu, Vishnu, Vishnu."

The Divine Test

Dhruv's extraordinary journey did not go unnoticed in the celestial realms. The devas (gods) watched in awe as this young child braved dangers that would make grown men quail. His unwavering devotion and single-minded focus created ripples in the cosmic order.

Intrigued and moved by Dhruv's devotion, the celestial sage Narada decided to test the boy's resolve. Disguising himself as an old wanderer, Narada appeared before Dhruv as he rested under a banyan tree.

"Child," Narada called out, his voice creaking with feigned age, "what are you doing all alone in this perilous forest? Don't you know these woods are home to fierce tigers and venomous serpents? Come, let me take you back to the safety of your home."

Dhruv looked up at the old man, his eyes shining with a wisdom far beyond his years. "Kind sir," he replied, his voice unwavering, "I thank you for your concern. But I cannot turn back now. I seek Lord Vishnu, and I will not rest until I find Him. No tiger is as fierce as my determination, no serpent as strong as my faith."

Narada, still in disguise, pressed further. "But child, you are so young. How can you hope to find the Lord when even great sages spend lifetimes in search of Him? Return to your parents. Enjoy your childhood. There will be time for spiritual pursuits when you are older."

Dhruv stood up, his small frame somehow seeming to tower in that moment. "Age is no barrier to devotion," he declared. "The Lord resides in every heart, young or old. I feel Him calling to me, and I must answer. I cannot return until I have seen Him with my own eyes."

Moved beyond words, Narada revealed his true form. The old man's visage melted away, replaced by the radiant countenance of the celestial sage. Dhruv's eyes widened in wonder, but he did not falter.

"Young prince," Narada said, his voice filled with admiration, "your faith has touched my heart. Truly, you are a soul of rare devotion. I will help you on your path." And with that, he taught

Dhruv a sacred mantra, a key to unlock the doors of divine perception.

The Tapasya

Armed with the sacred mantra imparted by Narada, Dhruv's meditation took on a new intensity. He found a serene spot in the heart of the forest, beside a gently flowing river. There, he began his tapasya (spiritual austerity).

Standing on one leg, his arms raised towards the heavens, Dhruv began to chant the mantra. Days passed, then weeks, then months. The scorching sun beat down upon him, but he did not seek shade. Torrential rains lashed at his small body, but he did not seek shelter. Bitter winds cut through the forest, but he did not shiver.

His body grew thin, his skin weathered by the elements, but the light in his eyes only grew brighter. The animals of the forest, sensing the divine energy emanating from this young ascetic, gathered around him. Deer grazed peacefully nearby, birds perched on his outstretched arms, and even the predators sat quietly, their fierce natures calmed in his presence.

As Dhruv's meditation deepened, extraordinary phenomena began to occur. The earth trembled beneath his feet, the rivers flowed upstream, and the stars in the sky danced in new constellations. The cosmic balance itself seemed to waver under the sheer force of his devotion.

In the celestial realms, the devas grew alarmed. The boy's tapasya was so powerful that it threatened the very foundations of the universe. They approached Lord Vishnu, beseeching him to intervene before the cosmic order was irreversibly disrupted.

The Divine Darshan

Finally, after what seemed like an eternity compressed into a moment, the forest was suddenly illuminated by a brilliant light. The air hummed with divine energy, and a heavenly fragrance permeated the atmosphere. Before the awestruck gaze of all creatures, great and small, Lord Vishnu himself appeared.

The Lord's form was resplendent, his four arms holding the conch, the discus, the mace, and the lotus. His eyes, filled with infinite compassion, gazed upon Dhruv. The young boy, sensing the divine presence, opened his eyes.

For a moment, Dhruv stood transfixed, his years of yearning culminating in this single, transcendent moment. Then, overcome with devotion, he fell prostrate at the Lord's feet, tears of joy streaming down his face.

Lord Vishnu gently raised Dhruv, his touch filling the boy with indescribable bliss. "Rise, my child," the Lord said, his voice resonating through the forest and echoing in the chambers of Dhruv's heart. "Your devotion has moved me. In all the worlds, I have never seen faith as pure and strong as yours. Ask, and whatever you desire shall be yours."

In that moment, as he gazed into the infinite depths of Lord Vishnu's eyes, Dhruv realized a profound truth. All his worldly desires – the longing for his father's lap, the wish for respect and recognition – seemed trivial and distant. He had found something far greater, a love that transcended all earthly bonds.

With folded hands, his voice choked with emotion, Dhruv spoke, "Oh Lord, I thought I wanted a place on my father's lap, a position of honor in his court. But now, having seen You, I realize that the only place I desire is a permanent one in Your heart. Grant me unwavering devotion to You, life after life."

Pleased beyond measure, Lord Vishnu blessed Dhruv. "My dear child, not only will you always have a place in my heart, but I grant you a place that will remain steadfast for all eternity. You shall become the Pole Star, fixed in the northern sky, around which all other stars will revolve. Kingdoms will rise and fall, epochs will come and go, but your position will remain unshaken, a testament to your unwavering faith."

With these words, Lord Vishnu vanished, leaving behind a transformed Dhruv. The forest, which had been his home and teacher for so long, seemed to bow in reverence to the young sage.

The Return and Beyond

Dhruv's return to the kingdom was marked by great rejoicing. King Uttanpada, consumed by remorse for his neglect, embraced his son with tears in his eyes. Queen Suniti's heart swelled with pride and joy at her son's spiritual achievement. Even Queen Suruchi, humbled by Dhruv's greatness, sought his forgiveness.

But Dhruv, though kind and forgiving, was no longer the same child who had left the palace. His eyes now held the wisdom of the ages, his words carried the weight of spiritual truth. He took his place in the court not as a prince seeking validation, but as a beacon of devotion and righteousness.

In time, Dhruv became king, ruling with justice, compassion, and spiritual insight. His reign was marked by prosperity and peace. But even as he fulfilled his worldly duties, his heart remained fixed on Lord Vishnu, every action a form of worship.

And when his time on earth came to an end, Dhruv ascended to the northern sky, becoming the Pole Star, Dhruva Nakshatra. There he remains to this day, a constant guide to travelers, a symbol of steadfastness, and an eternal reminder of the power of pure devotion.

Reflections on an Timeless Tale

The story of Balak Dhruv resonates across ages, offering profound insights that are as relevant today as they were millennia ago:

1. The Power of Innocence: Dhruv's journey began with a child's innocent desire for love and recognition. This purity of intent, untainted by worldly cunningness, became the foundation of his extraordinary spiritual achievement. In our complex, often cynical world, we would do well to nurture and value the innocence within us and around us.

2. Transformation of Desire: What began as a worldly desire for his father's affection transformed into a spiritual quest for divine love. This illustrates how, when pursued with sincerity, even ordinary desires can lead us to extraordinary spiritual growth. It encourages us to look deeper into our wants and aspirations, to find the spiritual longing that often underlies our material desires.

3. Persistence Against All Odds: Dhruv's unwavering determination in the face of

seemingly insurmountable obstacles – his tender age, the dangers of the forest, the rigors of ascetic life – serves as a powerful reminder that with true commitment, we can overcome any challenge. In our lives, when we face difficulties, we can draw strength from Dhruv's example.

4. The Equality of Divine Love: Lord Vishnu's appearance to young Dhruv demonstrates that divine grace is not reserved for the elderly, the learned, or the powerful. It is available to all who seek it with a pure heart. This democratization of spirituality is a powerful message in a world often divided by hierarchies and discrimination.

5. The True Meaning of Honor: Dhruv initially set out to gain honor in his father's court but found a place of unparalleled honor in the cosmic order. This teaches us to look beyond worldly recognition and seek that which truly elevates our soul. Sometimes, our greatest achievements come not from fulfilling our original goals, but from transcending them.

6. The Role of Guidance: The timely appearance of sage Narada in Dhruv's journey highlights the importance of spiritual guidance. Even the most determined seeker can benefit from the wisdom of those who have trodden the path before. In our own spiritual or personal growth journeys, we

should remain open to guidance and mentorship.

7. The Power of a Mother's Love: Suniti's role in Dhruv's story is pivotal. Instead of nurturing bitterness in her son, she directed him towards a higher purpose. This underscores the profound impact a parent's wisdom can have on a child's life direction. It reminds us of the responsibility we carry in guiding the younger generation.

8. The Transformative Power of Devotion: Dhruv's single-minded devotion not only transformed him but also affected the cosmic order, moving the gods themselves. This illustrates the incredible potential within each of us. When we commit ourselves fully to a noble purpose, we tap into a power that can reshape our world.

9. Forgiveness and Transcendence: Upon his return, Dhruv's forgiveness of those who had wronged him shows the transformative power of spiritual enlightenment. He transcended the cycle of hurt and revenge, embodying the highest ideals of compassion and understanding. In our lives, forgiveness can be a powerful tool for personal peace and social harmony.

THE STORY OF SAVITRI AND SATYAVAN FROM THE MARKANDEYA PURANA

The story of Savitri and Satyavan from the Markandeya Puranais one of the most profound and moving tales of love, determination, and the triumph of devotion over destiny. It speaks of the power of human will and the strength that comes from unshakeable faith and love. A tale that transcends time, it captures the very essence of what it means to defy fate in the name of righteousness and affection.

The Meeting of Fates:

In the ancient kingdom of Madra, there lived a princess named Savitri, renowned for her beauty, grace, and unwavering devotion to her father, King Ashwapati. Yet, more than her beauty, it was her intelligence and inner strength that made her stand apart from the other princesses of her time. Her father, eager to see her wed, left her free to choose her own husband, trusting in her judgement.

After a long journey seeking the right partner, Savitri found herself in a forested kingdom where she met Satyavan, the son of a blind, exiled king.

Satyavan was as noble as he was kind, living in simplicity with his parents, far from the grandeur of palaces. Despite the humble circumstances, Savitri was drawn to his pure heart and noble character.

However, there was a dark prophecy lurking in the shadows. The sage Narada, known for his foresight, warned Savitri of Satyavan's ill fate. He was destined to die exactly one year from the day of their marriage. The prophecy fell heavy on the hearts of those around her. But Savitri, undeterred, declared firmly, "I will marry none but Satyavan." For her, love was not something measured by time, but by depth. She believed that even one year with him was worth more than a lifetime with any other.

A Year of Bliss:

The days that followed their union were marked by joy, simplicity, and love. Savitri and Satyavan lived in the forest, tending to his ageing parents and living a life of contentment, away from the riches she had once known. Though she never spoke of it, the shadow of the prophecy never left her heart. With each passing day, the weight of Satyavan's impending death grew heavier.

When the fateful day approached, Savitri took a vow. She fasted and prayed, invoking all the powers she could summon to protect her beloved. Her mind was resolute, her spirit unyielding. She knew the battle ahead was not against man, but against destiny itself.

The Arrival of Yama:

On the day of Satyavan's death, the air was thick with an ominous stillness. Savitri followed Satyavan into the forest, where he went to chop wood, his usual daily task. As the sun climbed higher into the sky, a sudden weariness overtook him. He laid his head on her lap and, in moments, his life slipped away as if carried by the wind.

As Savitri sat holding Satyavan's lifeless body, the great Yama, the god of death, appeared before her. He came to claim what was his—Satyavan's soul. Yama, dark and formidable, was accustomed to being feared, his presence signalling the end. But Savitri, unflinching, followed him as he carried her husband's soul away. Her steps were deliberate, her resolve unwavering. She was not prepared to let go without a fight.

"Turn back, Princess," Yama warned. "Your husband's time has come. There is no power on earth or in heaven that can change what is destined."

But Savitri was not swayed. She walked alongside him, engaging Yama in conversation. She spoke of life and death, of righteousness and duty, and of the nature of love. Her words were filled with wisdom far beyond her years, and Yama, though determined in his task, began to listen.

In their journey, Savitri's eloquence became her weapon. She spoke of Dharma, the moral law that governs the universe, reminding Yama of the duty one has to righteousness and truth. "You, the lord of justice, must know the true power of love and devotion," she said. "A love like mine cannot be severed by death."

Impressed by her courage and wisdom, Yama granted her a series of boons. First, he restored her father-in-law's eyesight and kingdom. Then, he blessed her father with more sons to continue his lineage. But even after receiving these boons, Savitri continued to walk beside Yama, steadfast in her resolve. She knew that the only boon that truly mattered was the return of her beloved.

"Ask me no more, for no mortal may ask for the return of a soul already claimed," Yama warned once more.

But Savitri, ever astute, responded, "I have not yet asked for the life of my husband. But as you have granted me sons, how may I have them if my husband remains dead?"

Yama, bound by his own law, realised he had been outwitted. Savitri had not broken any rules, but rather used the gift of intellect and righteousness to achieve the impossible. The god of death, who had never been defied, found himself moved by her devotion. With great reverence, he returned Satyavan's soul to her.

The Triumph of Love:

As Yama disappeared into the shadows, Satyavan awoke, as if from a deep slumber. Savitri's joy knew no bounds, but it was a quiet, humble joy. She had not only saved her beloved but had reaffirmed the power of human determination, love, and the strength that lies within a heart that does not falter in the face of destiny.

The couple returned to their forest home, where Satyavan's parents awaited them with relief and astonishment. In time, Satyavan reclaimed his rightful place as king, and Savitri became a symbol of undying devotion and wisdom, her name immortalised in the hearts of those who heard her story.

Reflections:

The story of Savitri and Satyavan is more than just a tale of love. It is a lesson in the power of faith, courage, and devotion. Savitri's strength did not come from defiance but from her understanding of life's deeper truths. Her wisdom and adherence to righteousness became her armour, her love the driving force behind her actions. She teaches us that even in the face of death, when all seems lost, unwavering devotion and moral clarity can alter the course of fate itself.

It is also a reminder that while destiny may be written, the power of human will is immense. Through perseverance and righteousness, even the most insurmountable odds can be overcome. Savitri's journey with Yama is a metaphor for our own struggles with fate, and her victory is a testament to the belief that love, when aligned with virtue, transcends even death.

In the Markandeya Purana, this tale remains a shining beacon of hope for those who seek to overcome adversity. The strength of character that Savitri embodies speaks to the potential that lies within each of us—the potential to rewrite destiny when armed with love, wisdom, and devotion.

STORY OF MARKANDEYA : THE TALE OF DIVINE GRACE

The story of Markandeya from the Shiva Purana is one of the most stirring tales of divine grace, human devotion, and the mysterious interplay between fate and faith. It explores the delicate relationship between life and death, weaving together the themes of unconditional surrender, divine intervention, and the triumph of unwavering devotion. As we dive into the story, we find that it is more than just an account of a boy defying death—it's a testament to the transformative power of bhakti (devotion) and the eternal protection of Lord Shiva.

A Child Born Under the Shadow of Death:

In the kingdom of a pious sage named Mrikanda, there was sorrow rather than joy. Despite being a revered sage, Mrikanda and his wife Manasvani had been childless for many years. Desperate for a son, the couple prayed to Lord Shiva, performing severe penance to seek his favour. Touched by their devotion, Shiva appeared before them and presented them with a difficult choice: they could have a son who would be virtuous and wise but destined to die at the age of sixteen, or they could have a son who would live long but be foolish and unrighteous.

Without hesitation, the sage chose the former—a son of immense virtue, even if his time on earth would be brief. This decision was rooted in the understanding that life's quality, not its quantity, determines one's legacy.

Thus, the couple was blessed with a son, Markandeya, whose very name became synonymous with unshakable devotion. As the child grew, it became clear that he was no ordinary boy. Markandeya was blessed with wisdom beyond his years and a heart overflowing with devotion to Lord Shiva.

Markandeya's Devotion and the Looming Fate:

The years flew by, and as Markandeya approached his sixteenth year, the shadow of fate began to darken his life. The knowledge of his destiny—his impending death—hung over his family like an invisible sword. But young Markandeya, rather than living in fear, sought solace in his devotion. He spent every moment in prayer, meditating upon Shiva's form, finding peace in the divine presence.

In the days leading up to his sixteenth birthday, Markandeya's devotion only intensified. His love for Lord Shiva became his shield, and he immersed himself in the sacred mantra, "Om Namah Shivaya," surrendering his entire being to the deity. It was during one of these profound meditations that he encountered the ultimate test of his devotion.

The Arrival of Yama – The God of Death:

As the appointed hour of Markandeya's death arrived, Yama, the formidable god of death, descended upon the young boy. Yama's presence was inescapable, his duty non-negotiable. As he cast his noose to claim the boy's soul, Markandeya did something that startled even the god of death—he ran to the sacred image of Shiva and clung to the Shiva Lingam, wrapping his arms around it in total surrender.

"O Lord of serpents, Janardana, who controls the life of every being, protects me forever with your grace."

Markandeya's act of clinging to the Shiva Lingam symbolises his complete surrender. At that moment, he was no longer a boy awaiting his fate; he had become the embodiment of pure, fearless devotion. His attachment to the Shiva Lingam represents the soul's eternal quest to merge with the divine, defying the impermanence of life.

Yama, unfazed by the boy's devotion, cast his noose, but as the noose wrapped around Markandeya, it also encircled the Shiva Lingam. This was no ordinary moment. The noose intended to claim the boy had inadvertently insulted the Lord of the universe. Yama's overreach had awakened the very deity whom Markandeya worshipped.

The Emergence of Shiva:

In an explosion of light, the Shiva Lingam split open, and from its heart emerged the fierce, radiant form of Lord Shiva, eyes ablaze with fury. Shiva, the destroyer of all evils and protector of his devotees, stood between Yama and the boy. His wrath was palpable, his presence overwhelming.

"How dare you touch my devotee?" Shiva's voice thundered, shaking the heavens. "Markandeya is mine, and I protect those who surrender to me."

Yama, despite being the god of death, was powerless before the will of Mahadeva. With a single blow from Shiva's trident, Yama was vanquished. At that moment, death itself was subdued by devotion. Shiva, moved by the depth of Markandeya's love, granted him eternal life, making him immortal and ensuring that death would never touch him again.

"I grant you the boon, O blessed soul, for I am ever protective of those who take refuge in me. You have conquered death, and from this day forth, you will live forever."

In that divine proclamation, Shiva bestowed upon Markandeya not just immortality but also eternal refuge in his grace.

Reflections on the Story of Markandeya:

The story of Markandeya is not just a tale of defeating death; it is an allegory for the power of faith and absolute surrender. Markandeya's unwavering devotion teaches us that when we align our hearts with the divine and give ourselves completely, even the most feared forces in life, including death itself, become powerless before us.

This tale beautifully portrays the relationship between the devotee and the divine. It shows us that while death is inevitable for all beings, true bhakti (devotion) can transcend even the most unchangeable aspects of existence. Markandeya's clinging to the Shiva Lingam symbolises how the soul, when anchored in the divine, can rise above the transient nature of the world.

Moreover, the intervention of Shiva reflects an essential principle of the Hindu tradition: the grace of the divine is always available to those who sincerely seek it. Markandeya's fearlessness in the face of death was not born out of arrogance or defiance but from a place of pure love and trust. In that moment of complete surrender, Shiva's protection became inevitable.

This story also offers a profound lesson about the nature of destiny. Markandeya was born under the shadow of death, with the knowledge that his life was short. However, his devotion allowed him to transcend that destiny. It serves as a reminder that while fate may chart a path, it is not absolute. The force of devotion, when strong enough, can rewrite the course of destiny itself.

Conclusion:

Markandeya's tale remains timeless because it speaks to the deepest human longing: the desire to transcend the limitations of this world and be united with something eternal. His story reminds us that, in moments of our greatest fear or challenge, we can find refuge in faith. Shiva's protection of Markandeya is symbolic of the divine promise that no matter how dire our circumstances, devotion can transform our reality.

In the grand tapestry of the Shiva Purana, this tale stands out for its vivid portrayal of divine love, the power of devotion, and the ultimate triumph of the human spirit. It invites us to reflect on the nature of life, death, and the eternal bond that links the soul with the divine. Through Markandeya's unyielding devotion, we learn that even death, the ultimate end, can become a new beginning when we surrender ourselves fully to a higher power.

KING SHIBI'S ULTIMATE TEST: THE SELFLESS SACRIFICE OF A KING

In the ancient land of righteousness, where kings were seen not merely as rulers but as embodiments of virtue and protectors of Dharma, there was one monarch who stood as a beacon of compassion and justice. This is the tale of King Shibi, whose unparalleled devotion to his duty, humanity, and selflessness became a cornerstone of ethical teachings in the Vedic texts. His unwavering commitment to upholding Dharma, even at the cost of his own life, serves as a lesson for generations to come.

The Prelude: A Life of Dharma

King Shibi was a ruler of unmatched integrity, famed for his sense of justice and benevolence. His reign was marked by peace, prosperity, and fairness. People across the land revered him as the ideal king, one who treated his subjects as his children, always striving to ensure their welfare. His court was not just a place of political discourse but also a sanctuary for those seeking truth, justice, and protection. Word of his righteousness spread far and wide, reaching the ears of gods and sages alike.

But it is in moments of trial that a person's true character is revealed, and the gods sought to test the depths of King Shibi's virtue.

The Divine Test: A Call for Compassion

One day, the king was seated on his grand throne, listening to the grievances of his people when an unusual plea for help echoed through his palace. A dove, fluttering with fear, flew into the royal court and sought refuge on the king's lap. The dove was trembling, its heart racing as it sought the king's protection from an imminent danger. Just moments later, a mighty hawk swooped into the court, demanding that the dove be returned to him.

The hawk, with sharp eyes gleaming, addressed the king, "O mighty ruler! The dove is my prey, and by the natural law of the world, I have every right to claim it. Deny me my food, and you violate the very balance of nature."

The king, however, was a protector of all beings. He was bound by the Dharma to safeguard any living creature that sought his help. His heart brimmed with compassion for the helpless dove, but he also understood the hawk's argument— both creatures had a right to their survival.

King Shibi stood tall and responded with unwavering determination, "O noble hawk, I understand the laws of nature and respect your need to survive. However, I cannot forsake the life of this dove, which has sought refuge under my protection. I offer you a different solution. Instead of the dove's flesh, I shall give you an equal portion of my own flesh. This way, your hunger will be sated, and I will have kept my word."

The hawk, who was no ordinary bird but the god of fire, Agni, disguised in this form, was astounded by the king's offer. Yet, the test was not over.

The Sacrifice: A King's Flesh for a Dove

Without hesitation, King Shibi ordered his ministers to bring a pair of scales. On one side, he placed the dove, and on the other, he began to cut pieces of his own flesh to balance the weight. The dove, small and fragile, weighed little, but to the astonishment of all present, no matter how much flesh the king cut from his body, it did not match the weight of the dove.

The king, bleeding profusely yet steadfast in his resolve, continued to offer more and more of himself. As his courtiers and ministers watched in horror and admiration, King Shibi finally realised that the only way to tip the scales was to offer his entire body. His love for Dharma outweighed his concern for his own life.

"I shall offer my whole being," declared the king, "for the protection of this innocent creature."

The Divine Revelation: The Triumph of Dharma

At that moment, the hawk and the dove both transformed into their true forms—Agni, the god of fire, and Indra, the king of gods. They had come to test King Shibi's commitment to Dharma, and he had passed with flying colours. Not only had he been willing to sacrifice his own life for the sake of a humble bird, but he had done so without hesitation, driven purely by his sense of justice and compassion.

The gods, moved by his selflessness, healed his wounds and restored his body to its original state. They blessed him, declaring that his name would be immortalised as a symbol of ultimate sacrifice and righteousness. King Shibi's story was not just one of personal glory but a testimony to the power of Dharma, the force that holds the universe together.

The Reflection: The Inner Journey of Selflessness

King Shibi's tale resonates deeply within the teachings of the Upanishads, for it speaks of sacrifice, compassion, and the unwavering commitment to truth. The Upanishads emphasise the idea that the soul's ultimate purpose is to recognize its oneness with all beings. In Shibi's act of offering his own body for the life of another, we see the highest expression of selflessness, where the ego dissolves, and only the purest sense of duty remains.

His willingness to give his own life highlights the teaching that true strength lies not in power or wealth but in the capacity to serve others without expectation. The Upanishads teach that the Atman, the true self, is beyond the physical body, and Shibi's willingness to sacrifice his flesh underscores the insignificance of the material form when weighed against the eternal principles of Dharma.

King Shibi's ultimate test is a reminder to each of us that life's trials are opportunities for spiritual growth. In moments of challenge, when we are called to act selflessly, we tap into the deeper essence of our being—the part that is one with the universe, the part that transcends the limitations of the body and ego.

Through his story, we learn that true kingship is not about ruling over others but mastering oneself. The real test of a ruler—or any human being—lies in the ability to act with integrity, compassion, and a heart that embraces the well-being of all creatures.

Conclusion: An Eternal Lesson for Humanity

King Shibi's tale is a timeless reminder of the power of self-sacrifice and the profound spiritual truth that lies in serving others. His courage and commitment to Dharma exemplify the highest ideals of kingship, showing us that the greatest strength is not found in power but in love, compassion, and justice.

 In the end, King Shibi's sacrifice teaches us the Upanishadic wisdom that the self, when realised, transcends individual identity and merges with the cosmic order, for it is in giving that we find our true selves. His story continues to inspire, reminding us that in the ultimate test of life, it is our commitment to truth and virtue that defines us.

EKLAVYA: THE FORGOTTEN DISCIPLE'S UNWAVERING DEVOTION

In the sprawling forests of ancient India, a boy's determination to become the finest archer would lead to one of the most heart-wrenching tales of devotion and sacrifice. His name was Eklavya, and his story of dedication, despite being overshadowed by betrayal, still resonates as one of the most powerful examples of unwavering commitment and humility.

The Prelude: A Dream to Be the Best

Eklavya was the son of a tribal chief, living a simple life in the forest. Even as a young boy, he dreamed of mastering the art of archery. His heart was set on becoming the greatest archer, but there was a significant challenge ahead. At the time, the finest teacher in the world of archery was Dronacharya, the royal guru of the Kuru princes, including Arjuna, the best archer of his time.

Eklavya knew that if he wanted to excel, he needed to learn from the greatest. However, being from a humble background, he was aware that the path to Dronacharya would not be easy. Yet, his determination was unwavering.

The Denial: A Guru's Refusal

With high hopes, Eklavya made the long journey to meet Dronacharya at Hastinapura, the royal capital, where the great teacher trained the Pandavas and Kauravas. Upon reaching the royal grounds, Eklavya approached Drona with folded hands and humility, expressing his desire to learn the art of archery.

But Dronacharya, bound by the rigid caste and social norms of the time, refused to accept Eklavya as a student. He believed that his teachings were meant only for the royal family and nobility, not for a tribal boy. "I cannot teach you," Drona said firmly, rejecting Eklavya's plea.

The rejection was painful, but it didn't crush Eklavya's spirit. Instead of giving up, he decided to teach himself. If he couldn't have Dronacharya as his guru in person, he would still make him his teacher in spirit.

The Unseen Guru: A Statue of Dedication

Eklavya returned to the forest with a heart full of determination. He sculpted a statue of Dronacharya out of clay and set it in a quiet corner of the woods. Bowing before the statue, he declared, "You will be my teacher, Guru Drona, and I will practise in your name."

With that, Eklavya began his relentless training. Day and night, he practised his archery in front of the statue, imagining that Dronacharya was guiding him. His dedication knew no bounds, and over time, his skills grew sharper, rivalling even the finest archers in the land.

Through sheer willpower and self-discipline, Eklavya became an archer of extraordinary skill. He could hit his target with precision, his arrows flying with the accuracy of someone trained by the best.

The Encounter: Arjuna and Drona's Surprise

One day, Dronacharya and the Pandava princes, including Arjuna, ventured into the forest on a hunting expedition. As they moved through the dense woods, they came across a remarkable sight—an astonishing display of archery, with arrows piercing targets perfectly.

Curious, Dronacharya followed the source of the arrows, only to discover Eklavya practising in front of the statue. He watched in shock as the boy executed complex shots with a mastery that only a true disciple of his could display.

When Dronacharya approached Eklavya, the young archer greeted him with reverence. "I am your student, Guru Drona," Eklavya said humbly, bowing before him. "I have learned everything in your name."

Dronacharya was both impressed and troubled. He knew that Eklavya had become a powerful archer—perhaps even more skilled than Arjuna, his favourite disciple. This realisation troubled him deeply, for he had promised Arjuna that he would make him the greatest archer in the world.

The Unthinkable Sacrifice: Guru Dakshina

Troubled by the thought of Eklavya surpassing Arjuna, Dronacharya made a decision that would test the very limits of Eklavya's devotion. He approached the young archer and said, "If you truly consider me your guru, then I demand my guru dakshina (teacher's fee)."

Eklavya, with unshaken loyalty, replied, "Ask anything, Guru Drona. I will give you whatever you wish."

Dronacharya's next words pierced the silence like an arrow. "I ask for the thumb of your right hand."

For an archer, the thumb of the right hand is the most critical part of the body. Without it, the bow cannot be drawn, and the art of archery becomes impossible. It was a cruel and unimaginable request, one that would end Eklavya's dreams of being the greatest archer.

Yet, without hesitation, Eklavya unsheathed his dagger and, in a single, swift motion, cut off his thumb. He placed it at Dronacharya's feet, offering it as guru dakshina with the same reverence he had shown during his training.

Eklavya's act stunned everyone. Even Dronacharya, who had made the demand to protect Arjuna's future, was shaken by the depth of Eklavya's loyalty and sacrifice.

The Reflection: A Tale of Devotion and Injustice

The story of Eklavya is one of the most moving examples of selfless devotion in the Mahabharata. His unwavering respect for his teacher, even in the face of injustice, remains a powerful lesson in loyalty and humility. Despite being denied formal instruction, Eklavya rose to greatness through his sheer determination and respect for his chosen path.

However, his story also brings to light the harsh realities of societal norms and the injustices that existed in ancient times. Eklavya was a victim of the rigid caste system that denied him the right to learn because of his background. Even though he proved his worth through hard work, he was forced to sacrifice his talent to maintain the status quo.

Eklavya's sacrifice highlights the complexities of Dharma in the Mahabharata. Was Dronacharya right in asking for such a harsh guru dakshina to protect Arjuna's legacy? Or was it an act of injustice towards a boy whose only fault was his brilliance? These questions invite reflection on the nature of duty, loyalty, and the fairness of societal structures.

The Legacy of Eklavya: An Eternal Symbol of Dedication

Eklavya may not have become the greatest archer in history, but his legacy lives on as a symbol of unmatched dedication. His story reminds us that true greatness lies not only in skill but also in the strength of character, humility, and the willingness to make sacrifices.

In life, we may face challenges that test our devotion to our goals, much like Eklavya did. His story teaches us the importance of perseverance, even in the face of rejection, and the power of belief in one's self. Although Eklavya's thumb was taken from him, his spirit, dedication, and unwavering loyalty made him a hero in his own right.

Eklavya's tale continues to inspire, showing us that sometimes, the greatest victories are not those that the world acknowledges, but those won within the heart.

SHABARI'S DEVOTION: THE PUREST OFFERING OF LOVE

In the grand epics of ancient India, the story of Shabari, a humble devotee from the Ramayana, stands as a shining example of unwavering faith, unconditional love, and the boundless grace of the divine. Her life, filled with simplicity and devotion, reminds us that true spirituality is not about ritualistic grandeur but about the purity of heart and intention. Shabari's encounter with Lord Rama is one of the most poignant and moving tales in the Ramayana, a story of devotion that transcends all boundaries of caste, status, and knowledge.

The Prelude: A Simple Life of Devotion

Shabari was born into a tribal community, one that lived away from the grand cities and royal palaces of the world. Despite her humble background, she carried a burning desire in her heart to connect with the divine. Her heart, pure and filled with love, longed for nothing more than to serve a higher purpose.

From a young age, Shabari witnessed various rituals and sacrifices carried out by her people, often accompanied by the killing of animals. This practice disturbed her deeply, as her soul was filled with compassion for all living beings. Determined to seek a way of life that was in harmony with her gentle heart, Shabari left her village in search of a spiritual guide. She wandered into the forest, where her life's journey would take a divine turn.

The Meeting with Sage Matanga: A Life of Simple Service

In the heart of the forest, Shabari came across Sage Matanga's ashrama, a place where peace, knowledge, and devotion thrived. She fell at the sage's feet, asking for guidance and a chance to serve. Sage Matanga, seeing the purity in her heart, accepted her as a disciple. From that day onward, Shabari devoted her life to serving the ashram, performing simple tasks like cleaning, gathering fruits, and tending to the animals.

Though she did not have the intellectual learning of other sages and disciples, Shabari's devotion was her greatest strength. Her love for her guru and her longing for the divine was so deep that it caught the attention of Sage Matanga himself. Before he left his mortal body, he blessed Shabari and assured her that one day, the Supreme Lord Rama would visit her humble home.

"Wait patiently, my child," he told her, "for Lord Rama will come to you, and you will have the rare honour of hosting him."

With these words etched into her heart, Shabari continued her life of simple devotion, waiting for the day when her beloved Rama would arrive.

The Waiting: Years of Faithful Anticipation

Every single day, from the moment Sage Matanga left, Shabari lived with the hope that Lord Rama would visit her. She woke up early, cleaned her hut, decorated the pathway, and gathered the freshest fruits from the forest. She would then taste each fruit to ensure it was sweet enough for Rama. This became her daily routine for years, never doubting the words of her guru, never growing impatient.

Her heart, filled with devotion and faith, kept her alive with joy, even though she had no idea when or if Lord Rama would ever come. Despite her humble status and the fact that she lived in the wilderness, far away from the grand temples and cities where kings and priests performed elaborate rituals, Shabari's devotion was unparalleled. Her simplicity, humility, and love became her form of worship.

The Arrival: Lord Rama Visits Shabari

One day, as Shabari went about her daily routine of cleaning the path and gathering fruits, she saw two figures approaching in the distance. Her heart leapt with joy. She immediately recognized them—Lord Rama and his brother Lakshmana had come to her humble abode, just as her guru had foretold.

Shabari, overwhelmed with emotion, fell at Lord Rama's feet. She wept tears of joy, unable to contain her happiness. Lord Rama, seeing her pure heart and deep devotion, lifted her gently and spoke to her with great affection.

"Mother," he said, "your devotion has brought me here. I am pleased with your love and service."

Shabari, trembling with excitement, offered Rama and Lakshmana the fruits she had carefully gathered and tasted. Though the fruits were already bitten into, Rama, understanding the love with which they were offered, ate them with great delight. Each bite of the fruit was sweeter to him than the most elaborate offerings made in grand temples. For Lord Rama, it was not the fruit but the love behind the offering that mattered.

As Shabari served them, she asked Lord Rama for guidance. "My Lord, I am but an uneducated woman. I know little of rituals and scriptures. Please show me the way to attain your grace."

Lord Rama, deeply moved by her humility, told her, "True devotion, bhakti, does not require wealth, knowledge, or status. All that is needed is a heart full of love and faith. You have already attained the highest path, Shabari, by your unwavering devotion."

After blessing her, Lord Rama left with Lakshmana to continue their search for Sita, but Shabari's life was now complete. Her long years of waiting, filled with faith and love, had been rewarded with the darshan (holy sight) of Lord Rama. Her soul, filled with divine grace, was now at peace.

The Reflection: The Power of Devotion

Shabari's tale from the Ramayana teaches us one of the simplest yet most profound lessons—true devotion is about the purity of heart, not grand rituals or scholarly knowledge. Despite her humble origins, Shabari's love for Lord Rama was pure and unwavering. She waited for years, with complete faith in the promise of her guru, and her faith was ultimately rewarded.

In many ways, Shabari represents the essence of the bhakti (devotional) path, which is one of the central teachings of the Ramayana and the Upanishads. Her life shows us that the divine does not discriminate based on caste, wealth, or education. What matters most is the sincerity of one's heart.

Shabari also teaches us the importance of patience and faith. Despite living in the isolation of the forest, away from the world's grand events, she never gave up hope. She never grew weary of waiting, because her devotion sustained her. In our own lives, we often struggle with impatience and doubt, but Shabari's story reminds us that divine grace comes to those who are steadfast in their faith, even if the wait is long.

Her act of offering the half-eaten fruits to Lord Rama also carries a deep lesson. To the outside world, such an offering might seem inappropriate, but to the divine, it is the love and intention behind the offering that matter most. This teaches us that what we offer to the world—whether it's love, service, or kindness—need not be grand or perfect. What matters is that it comes from a place of sincerity and purity.

Shabari's story continues to inspire countless devotees and seekers, showing that true spirituality transcends all external barriers. Her life, simple and filled with love, stands as a reminder that the divine is not far away. The Lord resides in the hearts of those who serve with humility, wait with faith, and offer their love without any expectation.

In a world often obsessed with material success and social status, Shabari's tale reminds us of the beauty of simplicity, the power of devotion, and the eternal grace that comes to those who walk the path of love.

For a concluding chapter that ties together the depth and significance of your book on the Upanishads, you can focus on synthesising the main teachings while offering the reader a final reflection on their personal journey. Here's a suggestion for the concluding chapter:

THE ETERNAL JOURNEY: LIVING THE TEACHINGS OF THE UPANISHADS

As we come to the conclusion of this exploration of the Upanishads, it is essential to reflect on the timeless wisdom they offer and how these ancient teachings remain profoundly relevant in our modern lives. The Upanishads, with their subtle yet powerful messages, guide us toward the realisation that life is more than the pursuit of material gains or fleeting pleasures. They invite us to dive deep into the nature of existence, asking the most fundamental questions: *Who am I? What is the true nature of the self? What is the ultimate reality?*

In traversing the stories, dialogues, and profound teachings of the Upanishads, we have journeyed through layers of understanding, from the external world of appearances to the innermost core of our being—the Atman. This journey is not merely a philosophical pursuit but a call to transform our lives, to live with greater awareness, compassion, and alignment with the eternal truths.

The Unity of the Self and the Cosmos

One of the most enduring messages of the Upanishads is the unity between the individual self (Atman) and the ultimate reality (Brahman). The teachings remind us that the divisions we perceive—between ourselves and others, between the material and the spiritual, between the finite and the infinite—are mere illusions created by Maya. At the heart of existence lies the realisation of **Tat Tvam Asi**—"Thou art That." This truth is not just a lofty philosophical statement but a call to experience the oneness of all things.

In understanding this unity, we are invited to transcend the limitations of ego, pride, and desire. We are called to see the divine essence in ourselves and others, to recognize that everything we experience is a manifestation of the same ultimate reality. This shift in perspective allows us to live more harmoniously, with less attachment to the material and more alignment with the spiritual.

The Power of Inner Knowledge

Throughout this book, we have seen that the Upanishads do not seek to impart external knowledge or rituals but guide us toward an inward journey of self-discovery. The ultimate knowledge—the realisation of the self as Brahman—cannot be attained through intellectual pursuits alone. It requires introspection, meditation, and a willingness to look beyond the surface of life's distractions.

This inward journey, however, is not without its challenges. The ego, desires, and fears often act as barriers, keeping us tethered to a limited understanding of who we are. But, as the stories of Nachiketa, Uddalaka, and other seekers show, it is through perseverance, reflection, and the guidance of a guru that we can transcend these limitations and arrive at the profound knowledge of the self.

Living the Wisdom of the Upanishads

The teachings of the Upanishads are not meant to be confined to academic or intellectual study. They are living wisdom—meant to be practised, experienced, and integrated into daily life. The Upanishads encourage us to live with mindfulness, to question our attachments, and to seek a deeper connection with the world around us. They ask us to live with awareness of our true nature, embracing the unity of all existence.

In our everyday lives, we can embody this wisdom by practising compassion, cultivating humility, and nurturing our spiritual growth. Whether through meditation, contemplation, or acts of kindness, we are constantly offered opportunities to live in alignment with the truths of the Upanishads. Every interaction becomes a reflection of our inner state, and every moment becomes a step toward greater self-awareness.

The Timelessness of the Upanishadic Teachings

One of the most remarkable aspects of the Upanishads is their timeless relevance. Despite being composed thousands of years ago, their teachings continue to speak to the human condition—our struggles, aspirations, and search for meaning. The Upanishads remind us that while the world around us may change, the fundamental questions of existence remain the same.

In a world increasingly driven by materialism and superficial pursuits, the Upanishads offer a counterbalance. They call us back to what is eternal and unchanging: the self, the spirit, the divine essence that lies at the core of all things. They remind us that true fulfilment does not come from accumulating wealth or power but from understanding and experiencing the deeper truths of existence.

The Journey Continues

While this book may come to an end, the journey of self-discovery and spiritual growth is never truly complete. The teachings of the Upanishads are meant to be a guide—one that we revisit throughout our lives as we continue to evolve and deepen our understanding. The path of realising the self as Brahman is a lifelong journey, filled with moments of insight, challenge, and transformation.

As you close the pages of this book, remember that the wisdom of the Upanishads is not confined to the text. It is a living force, one that can be felt in every moment of life, in every breath, and in every experience. The journey to self-realisation is ongoing, and the Upanishads will always be there to guide you, whether through meditation, reflection, or the quiet moments of life when you pause to ask: *Who am I?*

In concluding this exploration, we return to the core message of the Upanishads: the self is not separate from the ultimate reality. The divisions we perceive are illusions, and the ultimate truth is one of unity, compassion, and eternal wisdom. By internalising these teachings, we can live more consciously, more peacefully, and more in harmony with the divine essence that connects us all.

May the wisdom of the Upanishads continue to unfold within you, and may your journey toward self-realisation be filled with clarity, insight, and a deep sense of peace. The truth is within you—**Tat Tvam Asi**